LAWLESS MACKINAC

Jennifer S. McGraw

Pine Stump Publications
St. Ignace, Michigan

© 2011 Pine Stump Publications

ISBN: 978-0-615-47028-3

Library of Congress Control Number: 2011931064

First Edition 2011

10   9   8   7   6   5   4   3

Published by Pine Stump Publications
St. Ignace, Michigan 49781

The cover art is used with permission of the Wisconsin Historical Society and is Image Number 2784, Marquette and Joliet Exploring the Upper Mississippi by Frank H. Zeitler, 1921.

Lawless Mackinac *is dedicated to my granddaughter, Jane Elizabeth St. Onge, who is a descendant of the Native Americans of the Straits area, the explorer Joliet, and early missionaries to the Native American Tribes in Michigan. May you grow up to be as adventurous, fearless, and independent as the people of the era.*

My appreciation to my husband, Chris McGraw, and kids, Zachary and Sydney Schroeder, for their kind attention and support. My thanks to Janette Nelson who edited the book and the kind people at Avery Color Studios who helped me print it. And thanks to the members of the Michilimackinac Historical Society who inspired my interest in early French and Native American history.

CONTENTS

FOREWORD

Americans treasure Wild West history. Words, names and phrases like Tombstone, OK Corral, gunslinger or Dodge City bring about visions of cowboys, gunfights and other related action and intrigue. Hidden behind a language barrier and 200 years older than the history of the Old West is the history of the really old west, the western outposts of the fur trade.

Michilimackinac, then located at the site of present day St. Ignace, was the western most outpost and the western capital of the fur trade. It was also the scene of murders, prostitution, embezzlement, arson, gambling and corruption.

Into this scene came Jesuit missionaries who were assigned the job of installing French morals into the Native Americans and French who lived at or visited this trading capital.

Also given the job of controlling the lawless masses were a series of French commandants, some unwilling and some as lawless or more so than the Jesuit's often uncooperative flock.

Of course, all of this took place when the Michilimackinac region was still a part of Canada. Written records were all in French, not English. This has caused our history to appear as

1

fractured fragments, one page or one paragraph at a time, in huge translated journals or textbooks.

It is in this way that I have collected and assembled the bits and pieces found within this document, pulling a paragraph from one source and comparing it to a translated version of another source.

After three years of research much of life at Michilimackinac is still a mystery. Questions still remain. I still do not know where Fort de Buade was located. I question if there were several forts. Was there a Fort Michilimackinac and also a Fort de Buade? Someday soon more French documents will be located and translated. More journals will be discovered in attics long covered in dust; and more mentally nimble history scholars will take interest in the area and time period. Then perhaps my questions will be answered.

In the meantime, this book is meant to give a glimpse into the fascinating French Colonial period of the Straits area when St. Ignace was the home base for exploration of an entire continent.

CALENDAR OF EVENTS

1500 - Near the turn of the sixteenth century the exploration of North America had begun. For decades prior, several nations had been fishing in the waters of eastern Canada. Centuries prior, the Vikings had a settlement on the shores of Newfoundland. Slave trade and the search for the non-existent passage to the Orient spurred the movement inland.

Trade in Native American slaves was common and soon became a prominent, lucrative secondary income for explorers, fur traders and fishermen.

1615 - Around the time Jamestown was founded by the English, Samuel de Champlain, Governor of Canada and explorer, discovered Lake Huron. Etienne Brule, a 19-year old scout for Samuel de Champlain, explored Canada, including parts of the Great Lakes. The Huron killed Brule in 1632. Little is known about his specific explorations.

1634 - Explorer Jean Nicolet, who was also employed by Samuel de Champlain, traveled through the Straits of Mackinac to Wisconsin searching for the passage to the Orient.

1635 - Coinciding with the first written accounts of exploration in the Great Lakes, the Native American population began to suffer. For example, between 1630 and 1640, the Iroquois population was reduced by half because of smallpox. By the end of the 1630s, the Huron population was reduced from 30,000 to 10,000 by small pox, measles and other European diseases. They also were slaughtered at the hands of the Iroquois, who had been given guns by Dutch colonists in New York.

1641 - Jesuit Father Charles Raymbault and Father Isaac Jogues built a mission on the rapids at Sault Ste. Marie, Michigan. They called this the Falls or Rapids of St. Mary. It was abandoned shortly thereafter.

1642 - Jean Nicolet could not swim and drown in a shipwreck near Sillery, Quebec.

1645 - Historians estimate there were 20 traders trading throughout the Great Lakes without government permission. These unlicensed traders were known as 'coureurs de bois' which literally translates as woods runners.

1648 – According to *French Limits in North America*, the memoir of Jacques Rene de Brisay, Marquis de Denonville, a Governor of New France in the 1680s,[1] the French occupied Michilimackinac at St. Ignace as early as 1648.

1649 – The Huron population dropped further due to warfare with the Iroquois. Estimates indicate the remaining Huron numbered only 1,000.

1661 - Louis the XIV became King of France. The French Monarchy became concerned for the first time with exploring and populating New France.

1665 - Bubonic plague ravaged London but did not deter Pierre Esprit Radisson and his brother-in-law Medard Chouart des Grossiellers, who were notable French traders. They traveled to England seeking and gaining the partnerships and permission necessary to trade under the English flag. Permission was granted in 1670 and the Hudson's Bay Company was established.

1668 - A Jesuit Mission and French settlement were founded at Sault Ste. Marie, Michigan. This became the oldest city in the Midwest. The mission was abandoned toward the end of the 1600s and the Jesuits relocated to the site of present day St. Ignace.

1671 - A mission was established among the Huron at Michilimackinac. The Jesuits named the mission St. Ignace de Michilimackinac after the founder of their order. The mission was destroyed that same year by the Iroquois.

1673 - Louis Joliet was an explorer, fur trader and student of the priesthood. He and Jesuit Father Jacques Marquette left Michilimackinac to find the Mississippi on May 17, 1673. Marquette died on the return trip and was buried on the shore of Lake Michigan near Ludington. Native Americans returned to the grave site in 1677, dug up the remains and returned the bones to Michilimackinac for burial.

1673 - According to early historian John Read Bailey, the first fort in the Mackinac region was constructed somewhere near the site of the City of St. Ignace in 1673 and was named Fort Michilimackinac.[2] Other historians disagree and numerous dates are stated, ranging between 1671 and 1690.

1677 - A second mission was constructed near the site of the City of St. Ignace. Jesuit Father Henri Nouvel took up residence in a bark chapel at the Odawa village, five miles west of St. Ignace. This mission was called St. Francis Borgia.

1679 – Sailing on the first ship to sail the Great Lakes, the *Griffin*, Robert LaSalle and Henri de Tonty arrived at Michilimackinac on August 27, 1679. Eventually they traveled down Lake Michigan and built Fort Miami at St. Joseph, Michigan. By the end of September 1679, the *Griffin* had been lost in Lake Michigan. No sign of the ship has been found to this day. LaSalle was killed by members of his crew in 1687.

1685 - Dutch and English traders attempted to attack Michilimackinac.

1686 - Fort St. Joseph in Port Huron, Michigan was built by Daniel Greysolon Duluth[3] on the strategically important narrow passage between Lake Erie and Lake Huron. Two years later, the fort at Port Huron, Michigan was burned to the ground by its commander, Louis Armand, Baron de Lahontan. The garrison was moved to Michilimackinac.

1691 - Historians report that between 140 and 200 coureurs de bois lived in the vicinity of Michilimackinac. The count likely included St. Ignace and the Odawa village at Gros Cap, five miles west of St. Ignace. It is reported that Metis,[4] French and Ojibwa lived in the vicinity along with Huron and Odawa.

1695 - According to Antoine Laumet de Lamothe Cadillac, who was commandant of Fort de Buade from 1694-1698, sixty bark cabins lined the shore of St. Ignace.

1698 - Governor of New France, Louis de Buade, Count of Frontenac, passed away amidst falling fur prices. King Louis XIV ordered Fort de Buade abandoned.

1701 - The Great Peace of Montreal was signed by the French and 39 Native American tribes. The treaty signers included the Huron, Algonquins (Odawa and Ojibwa) and the Nations of the Iroquois, historic arch enemies of the Michilimackinac area tribes. Warfare that had lasted for nearly 100 years ended, but only temporarily.

In the same year Cadillac founded Detroit and lured most of the Huron away from St. Ignace. Only 25 Huron remained at Michilimackinac. Said Cadillac in 1703, "Thus only about twenty-five of them remain at that place, where Father de Carheil,[5] their missionary, remains ever resolute. This autumn I hope finally to tear this last feather from his wing; and I am convinced that this obstinate vicar will die in his parish without having a parishioner to bury him."[6]

Thus escalated the tug of war between the Jesuits and Cadillac for the bodies and souls of the Native Americans from Mackinac. Cadillac offered every inducement, attempting to lure the Natives to Detroit. At the same time the Jesuits complained to higher authorities in Quebec, seeking directives to reestablish Mackinac.

Between 1703 and 1706 - Jesuits burned their mission to the ground and left Michilimackinac, temporarily defeated. They maintained a seasonal presence at St. Ignace.

Between 1706 and 1708 - Jesuit Father James J. Marest was asked to return to St. Ignace by the Governor General of Canada, who promised immediate reestablishment of the garrison.

1708 - After a fire in the Odawa village the tribe began to relocate to Mackinaw City.

1714 - The Mission of Michilimackinac was permanently moved across the Straits to Mackinaw City. Shortly thereafter, Fort Michilimackinac was built on the south side of the Straits of Mackinac.

1759 - Quebec was lost to the British and American forces.

1760 - Montreal fell. New France was lost to the British. The next year, after 150 years of French rule in Michigan, British soldiers occupied Fort Mackinac.

INTRODUCTION

G laciers covered the Great Lakes Basin 10,000 years ago. Eventually, they began to melt and recede. Water from melting ice filled to capacity the depression that now contains Lake Michigan. Overflowing water ran eastward and formed an underground river which drained this body of water that is now referred to as Lake Michigan into what is now Lake Huron. The water rose for 5,000 years until only the top of Mackinac Island and the limestone cliffs around St. Ignace were visible. Gradually, rising water surpassed the present shoreline of the Great Lakes by miles. The water then subsided and eventually, about 3,000 years ago, stabilized to its present position.

Eventually, the cave encompassing the underground river between the two bodies of water collapsed. The narrow passage that formed when the cave gave way became the course of the Straits of Mackinac, now spanned by the Mackinac Bridge.

Rock formations called stacks, such as Castle Rock, are the oldest remaining landforms from this time period. Shallow, horizontal sea caves in these rock formations are evidence of the water lapping on the shores centuries ago. Ancient Native Americans[7] believed these caves and cliffs to be sacred places. They placed the bones of their ancestors in crevices and caves, making sacrifices to honor the spirits within the stacks.[8]

Defensive foxholes can also be found in the hilltops surrounding St. Ignace. The Natives were always mindfully watching for their enemies, the Iroquois from the east.

Fear of the war-loving Iroquois predicated the decision by the Huron Indians, who once lived east of Lake Huron, to move from the east and eventually locate at Point St. Ignace. Living among the Huron was Father Marquette, a French Catholic missionary of the Society of Jesus. Missionaries of the Society of Jesus were known as Jesuits.

The written history of the Michilimackinac region began with the arrival of Father Marquette in 1670.[9] It is believed by some that the first French visited Michilimackinac in the 1620s and inhabited the area by the 1630s. Specific reports of French in the region began in 1641 when the French planted a flag in Sault Ste. Marie, Michigan and claimed the territory as their own while numerous unimpressed Native Americans observed. The first specific statement describing the initial French occupancy at Michilimackinac was made by Jacques Rene de Brisay, Marquis de Denonville who was governor of New France in the 1680s. He stated there was a French trading post at Point St. Ignace as early as 1648. That was twenty years before Jesuit Father Jacques Marquette first arrived at Michilimackinac and built a mission where the Huron, Odawa and Chippewa Indians resided. Soon after the mission was built, the Huron and Odawa moved further west to Wisconsin to avoid the Iroquois. Marquette went with them to Chequamegon Bay, Wisconsin (near the Apostle Islands).

While living in Wisconsin the Odawa frequently skirmished with the Dakota[10] Tribe. The Dakota offered to make peace in 1669 but the Odawa killed and ate the peace envoys. In retaliation the Dakota captured and burned alive the Odawa Chief Sinago, who was responsible for the killings. Within a short period of time the Huron and Odawa found the Dakota too much to handle. They returned to the Michilimackinac region in 1671 and took up full-time residence on the north side of the Straits of Mackinac at St. Ignace. Marquette followed.

Though they were still being attacked by the Iroquois, St. Ignace provided greater numbers. The presence of the Ojibwa, who occupied the St. Ignace area from 1650 to 1685, helped to reinforce the safety of the Huron and Odawa. The Jesuits found a higher concentration of available potential converts.

The Jesuits attached a religious prefix to the Native American name for the area, calling it St. Ignatius de Michilimackinac. Typically the location was referred to as Michilimackinac or Mackinac for short. The term was used to describe the entire region and also to describe the village. Point St. Ignace was known by the Native Americans as the Point of the Iroquois Woman. Decades prior, a fierce battle had taken place between the local Native tribes and the Iroquois. Oral history described the southern point of the peninsula that St. Ignace lies upon as being the home of an Iroquois woman, the sole survivor of that battle. The bay now known as East Moran Bay was formerly known as Nadowa-Wikweiamashong or Bay of the Huron. Bishop Baraga referred to the bay as Bad Bay of the Iroquois Woman.

Marquette remained at Michilimackinac until 1673 when he left St. Ignace with Louis Joliet and five Miami Indian guides to find the Mississippi. During his return in 1675 Marquette became ill and died. His body was buried on the shore of Lake Michigan near Ludington, Michigan.

In 1677 a brigade of Kiskiskons (Odawa), Chippewa, Huron and Iroquois located Marquette's body, removed the remaining meat from the bones in the Native American tradition and returned with the bones to St. Ignace. They buried his bones in a birch bark box beneath the floor of the chapel.

"Accordingly, they opened the grave and uncovered the Body; and, although the flesh and internal organs were all dried up, they found it entire, so that not even the skin was in any way injured. This did not prevent them from proceeding to dissect it, as is their custom. They cleansed the bones and exposed them to the sun to dry; then, carefully laying them in a box of birch-bark, they set out to bring them to our mission of St. Ignace."[11]

Burial beneath the floor of a chapel was a great honor for Europeans, though this chapel was built not of marble and stone but log and bark.

The mission at St. Ignace became not only the burial place for Father Marquette but the centerpiece for the most prominent trade village in the Great Lakes.

THE VILLAGE

The village of St. Ignace consisted of a French section of sixty houses, the village of the Huron and the village of the Odawa in the late 1600s.

"This village is one of the largest in all Canada. There is a fine fort of pickets and sixty houses that form a street in a straight line. There is a garrison of well-disciplined, chosen soldiers, consisting of about 200 men, the best formed and most athletic to be found in the New World; besides many other persons who are residents here during two or three months in the year."[12]

By the 1660s orders were issued to prepare for the great cities which were destined to develop in the colony of New France. Street alignment was a major concern of the colonial government.

"The houses are arranged along the shore of this Great Lake Huron and fish and smoked meat constitute the principle food of the inhabitants." [13]

"The villages of the Savages,[14] in which there are six of seven thousand souls, are about a pistol shot distant from ours. All the lands are cleared for about three leagues[15] around their

village and are perfectly well cultivated. They produce a sufficient quantity of Indian corn for the use of both the French
and Savage inhabitants."[16]

Though only decades after the first explorers from Europe
laid eyes on the Michilimackinac area, life at Michilimackinac was as comfortable as a French frontier town could get.
In fact it was often described as a resort for the fur traders
and explorers of New France. They stopped to replenish
supplies or even to winter in the area.

Food was the most plentiful of any area west of Montreal. The
natural protection from the Iroquois to the east and the Dakota
to the west was geographically unmatched. Housing was available to protect traders from the extreme Great Lakes winters.

French houses were made of logs. Cadillac stated that the
houses of the French at Michilimackinac were created with
horizontal logs; perhaps the first horizontal log homes built
in what would later become the United States.

Building a log cabin required a great deal of work with an
ax. Straight logs were selected, cut to the proper size and
squared with an ax. Dovetail notches were cut into the end
of each log. The logs were lifted and dropped into place by
corner men and then additional notches were cut to hold the
next log. Holes for the chimneys, doors or windows were cut
out after the structure was erected. The logs were chinked
with moss, animal hair, mud or clay.

After the log structure reached a height of 7 to 8 feet, poles
were installed to support a second floor.

Nails were not used. The buildings were held together by
wooden pins called trunnels.

Door hinges could be made of wood and hung with wooden pins, or hinges could be made of heavy leather. Some cabins had doors which simply sat in front of the openings.

Chimneys were usually made of small hewn logs. The spaces between the logs and the inside of the chimney were plastered with clay mixed with cattail down. This hardened with use and worked quite well.[17]

Roofing materials included cedar bark or straw. The Jesuit house was roofed with boards. Ceilings were generally only high enough to permit standing, with no additional headroom.

Cabin floors were hard-packed dirt or half log puncheons, logs that had been split with an ax. Furs were likely used to cover the floors.

Large fireplaces were used for heating and cooking. Most villages in New France also had outdoor and often centralized, beehive bake ovens. These were shared by the French colonists who were known as habitants.

Furniture was made from rough-hewn planks, stretched hides or leather straps.

Only the homes of the wealthy in New France had glass windows because glass had to be imported. At times windows were covered in stretched, scraped fish skin or oiled paper. Lanterns or bundles of sticks fueled by bear grease, pine pitch or tallow provided lighting for dark indoor spaces.

The lower floor most likely was used as a common room where activities involving the family took place. Attic spaces provided storage areas or perhaps sleeping areas for children or servants.

Houses constructed using these techniques still stand in the St. Ignace area. Often the existence of the log walls is unknown until a remodeling project brings to light the hand-hewn logs and dovetailed corners.

White plaster was used for chimneys, fireplaces and exterior covering on French constructed buildings. Later accounts indicate remnants of the plaster could be seen for more than a century. Plaster, lime or whitewash covered all French residences because the lack of such coverings indicated deep and unacceptable poverty.

"...Also found in the possession of the present priest of St. Ignace, Father Jaoka (pronounced Yocca), a pen and ink sketch, on which I looked with most intense interest. This invaluable drawing gives the original site of the French village, the 'home of the Jesuits,' the Indian village, the Indian fort on the bluff and, most important of all, very accurately defines the contour of a little bay known as Nadowa - Wikweiamashong - i.e., as Mr. Jacker gave it, Nadowa Huron. Wik-weia - Here is a bay. Anglice - 'Little bay of the Huron;' or according to the [Chippewa] dictionary of Bishop Baraga, 'Bad bay of the Iroquois [woman].' Of the Indian village there is no trace. Their wigwams, built only of poles and bark, have not left a single vestige. Not so with the French village. You may still see the remains of their logs and plaster and the ruins of their chimneys."[18]

French habitants were granted long ribbon farms. Ribbon farms were tracts of land with small amounts of lake frontage, with acreage in the rear, stretching as far as a man could walk in a day. The idea was to provide waterfront in order to support canoe based transportation and sustenance fishing. Also provided were grazing, farming and wood cutting areas.

The typical width of a ribbon farm was 192 feet to five times that amount.[19] Today the ribbon farms, now known as Private Claims, are the basis for the division of property that make up the City of St. Ignace.

The cabins of the Native Americans were made from poles bent to form semi-circular shaped structures. Additional poles were then laced into the structure and the building was then covered by bark. These cabins were estimated to reach 130 feet in length and were typically 20 to 25 feet wide and 20 feet high. Platforms were installed within the cabin. There were no windows in the Native American cabins, only a hole in the ceiling to let out the smoke. Cabins would house several families.

Throughout New France, extreme fear of fire sweeping through villages promoted cautious practices. As early as the 1630s entire villages had been lost to fires. If the food supplies were also lost the results could be disastrous. The French were limited from smoking in public or even carrying tobacco. Hay could not be stored in homes.

Commanders of Fort de Buade reported to leaders in the East that the Native American cabins were laid out in straight lines like any European village. This was important during the formation of the colony, as future growth would require properly developed roads and logical property lines.

Many roads in St. Ignace still maintain names relating to the French Colonial era. These include Pointe La Barbe Road, Portage Road, Gros Cap Road and Marquette Street, which could be the oldest road in the Midwest.

THE MISSIONS

*J*esuit Relations, a 10,000 page collection of writings of the early Jesuits, discusses life at St. Ignace and the nearby village at Gros Cap. Throughout the collection, the Jesuits describe St. Ignace as the largest and most successful mission in the Great Lakes. The village of St. Ignace was a rendezvous and resort for traders. The centerpiece of St. Ignace de Michilimackinac was the Huron Mission.

"The island was known to Champlain before 1612… about 1669 the island of Michilimackinac,[20] so famous from position and commanding prominence, gave name to an extensive province of which was the emporium and capital and probably the first settled place in Michigan."[21]

The missions at St. Ignace were identified by the Native American tribe that each mission serviced.

The first and most often described mission was the Huron Mission. The most prevalent opinion seems to be that the Huron Mission existed as currently identified at the location of the Marquette Mission Museum, on the corner of Marquette Street and North State Street in St. Ignace, at the head of East Moran Bay. Not all historians agree on this location.

The most original opinion is that stated in *Michigan, A History* by Bruce Catton. Mr. Catton believed the mission was on top of Castle Rock.

"Apparently, the mission had been built on a flat-topped hill or butte at a place called Castle Rock, three miles north of the present town, with the fort at the mouth of a creek a mile south of the mission."[22]

Early historian Henry Schoolcraft was U. S. Indian agent for the area in the 1800s. He formed an opinion that the mission was on the bay after traveling to St. Ignace by canoe.

"We went on under a press of sail last evening until eight o'clock, when we encamped in a wide sandy bay in the Straits of Mackinac… On looking about, we found in the sand the stumps of cedar pickets, forming an antique enclosure, which, I judged, must have been the first site of the Mission of St. Ignace, founded by Pierre Marquette, upwards of a hundred and eighty years ago. Not a lisp of such a ruin had been heard by me previously. French and Indian tradition says nothing of it."[23]

The Huron Mission was first built around 1670, very near the site of a fortified Huron village. Early missions and villages were prone to destruction by fire. The Iroquois burned the Huron Mission and village in 1671 when the Senecas (Senecas are part of the Iroquois federation) attacked St. Ignace and other nearby villages.

A new mission house was constructed. A 25' palisade surrounded the new structures.

"On the supposed site of the house of the Jesuits… are found distinct outlines of walls, a little well and a small cellar. Immediately in the rear of the larger building are the remains of a forge, where 'the brothers' used to make spades or swords, as the occasion might require."[24]

A blacksmith shop was said to be located in the rear of the chapel. Tools as well as trinkets, used as rewards for attendance or pious acts, were manufactured. The ability to work metal was recognized by the Jesuits as a plus. They could provide services to the Native Americans such as tool manufacturing or repair and also produce rings, bells and crosses to delight potential converts.

By 1677 there were two missions in the St. Ignace area. The Huron Mission was located as previously discussed. The Kiskakon Mission ministered to the Odawa and other Algonquin speaking tribes and was located near the site of the Gros Cap Cemetery, five miles west of St. Ignace. This location was known to be the site of a fortified village. At some point in time it was also a trading post, owned by the trader Moran for which the Moran Bays and River were named.

"Father Nouvel took lodging, at the close of the month of November in the year 1677, in a small bark cabin, situated between the village of the Kiskiskons and the new village of the Outaouaks. It was distant three-quarters of a league from the mission house in which we usually live and where the church of St. Ignace stands, which does service for the Huron, especially in winter, at which time our Algonquins cannot assemble."[25]

"We had erected a small bark church adjoining our cabin, in which, when we wished to escape the smoke, the cold would not permit us to remain long. It was dedicated to St. Francis de Borgia, who was the first of the superiors of the Society who sent gospel workers into America..."[26]

The Kiskiskons or Cut Tails were part of a larger group of resident Algonquin speaking Odawa Tribes that also included the Sable Nation, the Sinago and the Nassauakuetoun, or Nation of the Fork. At times the Odawa were referred to as Upper Algonquins. They were more numerous and more influential than the Huron.

Though reports to Superiors regarding the Huron Mission seemed positive; the Odawa seemed less interested in conforming.

"The nation of the Outaouaks Sinagaux is far from the kingdom of God, being above all other nations addicted to lewdness, sacrifices and juggleries. They ridicule the prayer and will scarcely hear us speak of Christianity. They are proud and undeveloped and I think that so little can be done with this tribe, that I have not baptized healthy infants who seem likely to live, watching only for such as are sick... The Indians extremely attached to their reveries had resolved that a certain number of young women should prostitute themselves, each to choose such partner as she liked. No one in these cases ever refuses, as the lives of men are supposed to depend on it."[27]

The Jesuits lacked understanding of Native American courtship customs. This is shown in the quote above. The quote below shows the inability of the Odawa to understand the Jesuits. The Jesuits planted a Cross within the Kiskakon village. The Native Americans were riled by the Cross and explained that their enemies from the West, the Sioux or Dakota, used crosses when putting prisoners of war to death.

"We planted it on the Saturday before passion Sunday... There were only a few Frenchmen, himself and another savage who honored the Cross by a volley from their guns. All, however, were present at the pious act and the infidels joined with the Christians in venerating the Cross. That evening, the same two infidel Savages came to us; and, having expressed their pleasure at the planting of the Cross and their regret that their young men had not honored it by the discharge of their firearms..."[28]

Jesuit Relations indicates that a number of French occupied the Gros Cap area with the Odawa, and attended religious services at St. Francis Borgia. The French traders living in the village attempted to smooth the waters. They arranged for a second assembly to properly honor the cross. After prayers and hymns some of the Native Americans took out their guns, leading the Jesuits to believe they were shooting volleys in salute. Instead the mischievous Native Americans shot the cross, knocking parts off. The Jesuits were displeased.

"In few but strong words, we made them understand the infamy of the act and we abruptly withdrew into the Chapel. The door was at once closed upon every one. Our Savages seemed struck with consternation and we could not refrain from permitting to come into our Cabin at least a few of the most distinguished men of all the Nations, who came to us to express the mortification that they felt at an insult which we had so deeply resented. 'I rightly told thee,' a Kiskakon, who is not yet a Christian, said to me, 'That we live in this country like dogs, without order or rule.' We found, the next day at dawn, that all had been mended... An Infidel remarked that all felt that the murder of an Iroquois and of another stranger from the Loup Nation, which had been committed at the close of the autumn, had been a weighty affair; but that it was a trifling matter compared to the deed done in outraging the Cross of Jesus Christ... The children call each other to account, if anyone throws a stone in the direction of the Cross and they go to pray to God at the foot of the Cross, especially when the church is closed."[29]

The cross was repaired and a fence was built around it.

The location of the St. Francis Borgia Chapel is an unsolved mystery. As indicated in previous statements, the chapel was three-quarters of a league distant from the Chapel of St. Ignace de Michilimackinac, and between the village of the Kiskiskons and the new village of the Outaouaks.

Jesuit Relations 62, explains more regarding the term Outaouc. The quote below illustrates how confusing historic writings are when describing the Odawa.

"In the Outaouc Missions we include not only the Outaouacs or Upper Algonquins, who are divided into several tribes, namely: The Saulteurs, who usually dwell at Sault de Ste. Marie, at the entrance of Lake Superior; The Kiskiskons and three other tribes, all of whom have their own chiefs, at Saint Francois de Borgia, at the Junction of Lakes Huron and Illinois, at a place that we call Michilimackinac; The Nipissiriniens and other petty tribes on Lake Huron. We also include the Huron who reside at St. Ignace, three-fourths of a League from St. Francois de Borgia; The Outagamis and the Sakkis; The Pouteouatamis along the Bay des Puants, in a south-westerly direction from Michilimackinac; The Makoutens and the Oumiamis; The Kischigamins, along Lake Illinois; and the Illinois themselves, as we more nearly approach the South. We have houses with chapels at Sault de Ste. Marie, at St. Ignace, at St. Francois de Borgia and at St. Francois Xavier, at the extremity of the Bay des Puants wherein we perform with entire freedom all the exercises of religion and whence the missionaries frequently go on journeys among the surrounding nations."[30]

A portage likely followed the high ground from St. Ignace to the Odawa village at Gros Cap, nearly along Old Portage Road. Historians theorize that passage to the Odawa village was also made by canoe travel through Chain Lake, which was once known as Crane Lake, through Frechette Lake and down the Moran River.

"It was not exactly on the present Portage Street and Road as has been supposed for years, but started at East Moran Bay, went over the hill past the fort field and continued to the upper end and of what is now Goudreau Street. From there it continued along the ridge, veered northerly at one point and came out on the creek, now called Moran River. This runs through the Greenless[31] property and adjoins the historic cemetery."[32]

Though most quotes recognize and describe two chapels at Michilimackinac, a handful of historians believe there were three. A third chapel is reported to have been located in the Rabbit's Back area, north of St. Ignace. To date, specific quotes by more modern authors can be identified but no quotes from the period were found.

"There was an Algonquin village (various Odawa clans and Chippewa or Ojibwa) near Rabbit's Back at about the same time as the Gros Cap Settlement, or possibly before that time. A mission house was built there in 1673, as well as a dwelling house for the missionary. Father Hennepin who came with LaSalle is reported to have said Mass there. It is reported that in 1677 there were 1,300 Indians in the Rabbit's Back area."[33]

In the book, *Annals of Fort Mackinac*, Dwight H. Kelton expressed a similar opinion.

"...several clans of Ottawa and kindred tribes - all comprised by the missionaries under the name Algonquins - made their appearance and settled on the shore of Lake Huron, a little over 2 miles from the Jesuit's residence, accordingly near the bluff called by the Indians the She Rabbit, south of the He Rabbit, or Sitting Rabbit (Rabbit's Back). Here too a church and a dwelling house for the Ottawa missionary, were built."[34]

A quote from *Mackinac Formerly Michilimackinac* regarding LaSalle's arrival with the *Griffin* seems to confirm another chapel north of St. Ignace.

"We lay between two different nations of Savages. Those who inhabit the Point of Michilimackinac are called the Huron; and the others who are about three or four leagues more northward, are Odawa. Those Savages were equally surprised to see a ship in their country; and the noise of our cannon, of which we made a general discharge, filled them with great astonishment. We went to see the Odawa and celebrated mass in their habitation. M. LaSalle was finely dressed, having a scarlet cloak with broad gold lace and most of his men with their arms, attended him. The chief captains of that people received us with great civilities, after their own way and some of them came on board with us to see our ship, which rode all that way in the bay or creek I have spoken of. It was a diverting prospect to see, every day, above six score of canoes about it and the Savages staring and admiring that fine wooden canoe, as they called it. They brought us abundance of whitings and some trouts of fifty or sixty pound weight."[35]

As previously discussed, the mission at St. Ignace was attacked and burned in 1671. The Jesuit Mission in Sault Ste. Marie was also burned in the 1600s. The Jesuits were always in a great deal of peril, although those at Mackinac seemed to be physically safer than those at other missions.

Father Etienne de Carheil, a prominent Jesuit in Michilimackinac history, was long stationed in St. Ignace. He had previously ministered to the Iroquois and found life with them dangerous.

"Father de Carheil had a struggle with another, who tried to bite off his nose and who would have succeeded had not the Father been adroit enough to throw him upon the ground. Thus this arrogance which is, as it were, the peculiar characteristic of this nation; Their ardor for war, in which they are sometimes engaged for two years at a time and from which they cannot keep aloof without passing for cowards an insult which, to them, is much more bitter than death..."[36]

Methods of torture, often applied against warriors of other tribes, were also turned upon French victims including the Jesuits. Torture techniques used against the Jesuits included ripping off fingernails, biting or burning off digits, burning skin with hot ax heads, being burnt alive, dowsing in boiling water and driving pointed stakes into areas of the body. Jean de Brebeuf, a Jesuit killed by the Iroquois in the 1640s, had parts of his body cut off, roasted and eaten in front of him.

After numerous death threats, Carheil left the Iroquois Mission for Michilimackinac. He spent over 15 years at the St. Ignace Mission, which was the headquarters of the western missions. Eventually the chapel was purposely burned by Carheil and Joseph Jacques Marest in the first decade of the 1700s. The Jesuits had a presence at St. Ignace de Michilimackinac for 33 years.

LAWLESS LAND AND FRENCH VALUES

In early New France, as well as other areas of North America, it was obvious that the Europeans were poorly prepared. Often they arrived in the fall with inadequate food and no available shelter. The death rate in European settlements was astounding. Only five of sixteen French survived in Tadoussac, the oldest village in Canada in 1599. Four out of five English died at Jamestown, Virginia in 1607. Hernando De Soto lost 700 out of a 1,000 Spanish settlers when he founded his North American colony.

During the first two decades of French presence in the Great Lakes region about half of the total population, both Native American and French, died from European diseases.

The French government could not grasp the differences between Europe and the harsh environment of New France and relied on misguided policies.

"One busybody wrote to the colonial Intendant that a bake-oven should be established in every seigneury and that the habitants should be ordered to bring their dough there to be made into bread. The Intendant had to remind him that in the long cold winters of the St. Lawrence valley, the dough would be frozen stiff if the habitants, with their dwellings so widely scattered, were required to do anything of the kind. Another martinet gravely informed the colonial authorities that as a protection against Indian attacks 'all the seigneuries should be palisaded.' And some of the seigneurial estates were eight or ten miles square!"[37]

A seigneury was a long skinny parcel of land. In New France such parcels were provided to landlords or seigneurs who were typically clergy, military officers, nobles or groups of habitants. The parcels were then leased all or part to members who were lower in the class system. These tenants farmed, built houses and generally developed the parcels. The King's Intendant granted the properties to the seigneurs and collected taxes.

Early French settlements suffered from many miscalculations. Settlements were located in areas where there was no fresh water or where food sources were limited, such as on islands. Livestock was imported by ship but people were unprepared to raise the livestock and handle situations such as calving. Ice, at times, proved to be a surprise. Being iced-in prevented ships from leaving areas in a timely manner. This resulted in leaving those on board unprepared with inadequate food and supplies. Scurvy wiped out whole populations, when simple prevention was understood for years by the Native Americans prior to the arrival of Europeans.

Near the time of Marquette's arrival at Michilimackinac, the European population of New France was about 5,870. However, the French settlers or habitants had developed little means of self-support.

Even after 100 years, almost no industry outside of the fur trade was evident. Very few agricultural advancements had been made. Less than 15,000 acres of land, or 15,862 arpents,[38] were being cultivated by Europeans throughout the colony. Food needs were still substantially supplemented by shipments from Europe.

The first Europeans who explored, traded and settled Michilimackinac were impeded by an unknowing government. Add to this Jesuit law that constantly tampered as they attempted to reign in the untamed coureur de bois culture, without success. Throughout the seventeenth century the Jesuits imposed, proclaimed or were given superiority over government officials. The habitants had no say, political activity was forbidden and congregating to discuss politics promoted severe punishment.

All books were banned by the Jesuits except those dedicated to religious devotions.

The Jesuits tried to instill French values in the Native Americans and promoted these values among the French. For instance, the Jesuits continually asked the Native Americans to allow their children to be educated and taught French manners. Female children were preferred as the Jesuits had concluded girls more easily conformed to instructions. The Native Americans responded by sharing their young on occasion, at other times they denied the requests. When tribe members were unwilling to give up their children but felt the pressure to conform they kidnapped children from adjacent tribes. Of course, this act fueled warfare.

The French government tracked the flow of goods in and out of the region. The European traders were tracked and licensed. They were forced to return East with certificates from the Jesuits testifying to their good behavior.

Various strange laws were passed which interfered in the sex lives of the habitants of New France. Likely the motive was to increase the European population of the colony. One law that was passed in 1654 required habitants to be in their homes by 9 pm.

Fines were assessed to fathers of unmarried men over 20 and unmarried women over 16.

People who did not have families were forbidden to trade with Native Americans (Metis were exempt).

The King's Pleasure or King's Dowry was established in 1665 allowing for a payment of twenty to fifty livres (a livre is equivalent to the value of one pound of silver) to be paid to any European male in New France who was married by age 20. The money was actually given in the form of gifts meant to jump start the household which likely included an ox, a cow, two pigs, a pair of chickens, two barrels of salted meat and 11 crowns in cash. Twenty to fifty livres was to be paid any female married prior to age 16. This dowry was established to increase the population and encourage migration. Both males and females were typically wed by age 18 with the average marriage age of a female in New France being 14 until the 1660s.

The French initially did not consider mixed marriages as contributing to the goal of increasing the population. The Metis were thought to be too desirous of freedom, hard to control and typically considered part of the Native American population.

France began importing women to New France in the 1660s. These women were called filles du rois or King's Daughters.

Approximately 770 filles du rois traveled by ship to Canada seeking husbands, on the request of government officials. Many were orphans but historians theorize many others were daughters of debtors, prostitutes, widows or runaway wives. Some were of higher breeding and were requested so that they might be married to officers. In 1665 officers of the Carignan Salieres Regiment, the military regiment in charge of keeping the Iroquois in check, were allowed first pick of the filles du rois.

Most imported women found husbands immediately. Approximately 40 were never married. The Iroquois captured at least one woman.

Officials of New France requested that these imported women be healthy and stout. Good health was necessary in order to perform physical labor and to withstand the harsh environment. The same officials requested that priests in France certify to each woman's piousness.

Laws forbid unmarried men from hunting, fishing or trapping until the filles du rois were married. These women were not allowed to divorce or leave their husbands.

King Louis the XIV instituted the baby bonus in 1669. To increase the population, the King agreed to pay the parents of 10 legitimate children 300 livres. If the family included 12 children 400 livres would be paid. To be eligible for the baby bonus no child could be committed to the Catholic Church as a priest or nun and no child could be illegitimate.

Jesuits demanded European females conform to standards of dress that they established. It was thought that a woman's arms, shoulders, throat and head should be covered or she was considered indecent.

Demands were made on the male population by the Jesuits too. Those found guilty of providing liquor to the Native Americans were excommunicated and executions were demanded.

In New France it was illegal to purchase certain items from a Native American. These items included guns, shot, powder, clothes being worn, a man's wife or his children.

The Jesuits believed that hunger was more often felt by Native Americans who practiced Pagan religions; and they determined death by hunger to be less likely for converted, Christian Native Americans.

Jesuits frequently expressed concerns about the sexual practices of the Native Americans. Lack of understanding and tolerance was shown for the practices of polygamy, trial marriages and nakedness. They believed the children of polygamists were subject to early deaths.

"Tis a comical sight, to see 'em running from shop to shop, stark naked, with their bow and arrow. The nicer sort of women are wont to hold their fans before their eyes, to prevent their being frightened with the view of their ugly parts."[39]

Jesuits refused to marry Native American women to French men at various points in time. Jesuits from Michilimackinac worked to make these mixed marriages illegal.

'Country marriage' is a term that means a marriage made without the supervision of a priest.

It became clear that the incentives given the French habitants to increase the population of the colony were not working. Authorities changed attitudes regarding marriage between Native Americans and the French. By this time Metis populated the Michilimackinac region.

Native Americans found the Jesuit practices odd. Historic manuscripts refer often to contempt, threats and actual taking of Jesuit lives.

"His zeal was so great that he preached continually to these infidels, to try to convert them. His executioners were enraged against him for constantly speaking to them of God and of their conversion. To prevent him from speaking more, they cut off his tongue and both his upper and lower lips. After that, they set themselves to strip the flesh from his legs, thighs and arms, to the very bone; and then put it to roast before his eyes, in order to eat it."[40]

It is reported the Huron, Algonquins (Odawa and Chippewa) and Iroquois repeatedly discussed the execution of the Jesuit priests. The Native Americans recognized that the diseases that spread through their villages coincided with the arrival of the Jesuits and other Europeans.

Various government officials were suspicious of the Jesuit's motives. The Jesuit priests were accused of refraining from teaching the Native Americans the French language in order to establish themselves as interpreters, while securing fur trade profits.

The Jesuits complained that the Native Americans taught them obscene words in substitution for everyday objects as they learned the Native languages; then laughed boisterously when the Jesuits used the words in everyday conversation.

Native American bathing practices were of concern to the Jesuits. The French felt one bath per year was adequate. In their minds sweat lodges were unhealthy and promoted illness.

They wished to dissuade the Native Americans from living nomadic lifestyles because it hindered religious instruction. The Jesuits did not realize the necessity of nomadic lifestyles to prevent starvation.

Native Americans were punished by the Jesuits for witchcraft and magic. The Jesuits, who believed in werewolves, magic and flying canoes, criticized Native American reliance on dreams. There was concern that they allowed their whole lives to be ruled by the meaning of dreams.

Magicians known as Jugglers acted as doctors and druggists. They dispensed herbs or roots to cure illness. When this failed they ordered dogs of specific colors to be sacrificed to the sun or moon. Often, the cures worked. Cadillac describes the Native Americans abilities as very clever and expert. They successfully treated burns, bites, frost bite and broken bones with secret remedies.

WOMEN AND MEN

In the late 1600s it was obvious that the Jesuits could not grasp or accept the fact that Native American women had more freedoms than French women. While French women in Montreal were being banned from religious services for showing skin on their necks and elbows, Native American women were sometimes observed in partial or total nakedness.

"Among the Chippewas: After their corn-planting, a labor which falls to the women and as soon as the young blades began to shoot up from the hills, it was customary for the female head of the family to perform a circuit around the field in a state of nudity. For this purpose, she chose a dark evening and after divesting herself of her machecota, held it in her hands dragging it behind her as she ran, and in this way compassed the field. This singular rite was believed to protect the corn from blight and the ravages of worms and vermin and to insure a good crop."[41]

The women sought to protect the crops because they were the owners of the cornfields as well as the cabins, furnishings, utensils and other property. Ojibwa women built the houses and also decided who could live in them. Ojibwa men typically lived with their in-laws. Property was passed from mother to daughter.

Native American women did most of the physical labor including farming, processing furs and gathering.

Trade routes were owned by the Native women and the French caught on fast. Marriage by a French man to a woman with a particular trade route could be of great advantage. Quite possibly this also led to polygamy on behalf of some French men. Native American tribes at Michilimackinac practiced polygamy as a part of their culture.

"A plurality of wives is allowed of, amongst several of the nations of the Algonquin language and it is common enough to marry all the sisters; this custom is founded on a persuasion, that sisters must agree better together than strangers. In this case all the women are upon an equal footing; but amongst the true Algonquins there are two orders of wives, those of the second order being the slaves of the first."[42]

Huron typically had only one wife. However, some Iroquoian tribes allowed multiple husbands. Huron widowers were expected to marry deceased wives' sisters. Widows might be expected to marry their husband's brothers or other male relatives but only if their initial marriage resulted in no children.

French women who were pregnant out of wedlock could be punished by death. Those women facing such a pregnancy hid the birth; often with the help of an underground network of midwives, poor widows or Native American women who would raise the children known as enfants du roi. Native

American women had more freedoms in general, but especially in choosing spouses and dissolving marriages. Divorce was simply a matter of agreement or perhaps a matter of the woman throwing the man's possessions out in the yard.

Another practice that baffled the Jesuits was that referred to as "trial marriage". Such a marriage could be ended at the woman's whim. Native American women were allowed to try out potential spouses before choosing to marry them.

Such marriages were for purposes other than business. Traders might be months or years between visits with their European spouses. No European women[43] were reported to be at Michilimackinac until the 1700s. Metis women were reported at Michilimackinac. Reports indicate the Couc sisters, who were Metis, accompanied their husbands on trade expeditions and were frequently at Michilimackinac.

THE FORTS

The greater St. Ignace de Michilimackinac area was the location of at least five forts or palisades in the late 1600s. Included were the Jesuit palisade, Fort de Buade, the palisaded Huron village, the palisaded Odawa village at Gros Cap and the Odawa fort on the hill in St. Ignace.

Near the Jesuit Mission in what is now downtown St. Ignace, near the shore, was the Huron village. The Huron village and Odawa village were described as being divided by a single, primitive palisade. The Odawa later began to build a fort described as being on the hill, ten to twelve hundred paces from the village area.

According to La Hontan, the Huron village and palisaded fort, constructed in 1672, was on level ground around the middle of East Moran Bay. It existed there until about 1702 when that tribe and other bands left for Detroit.[44] John Read Bailey described the location as such: "The Odawas fearing trouble with the Huron began to fortify the neighboring bluff, north and in back of what is now, 1895, Cliffside and vicinity. There are remains there of an earthwork, supposed to be of Indian origin and many of their spearheads, flints, stone hammers and other relics have been found thereabouts. On the premises at Cliffside, St. Ignace, there is an enclosure of seven acres, all the natural scenery (except the arched rock), that can be found on Mackinac Island. In the yard, near the dwelling, there is a rock of the same formation as the island Sugar Loaf, but not quite as broad at the base. It is the Temple or Ghost rock - Gebi-wau-beek or Chete - of the Indians and in front there is a flattened projection - their alter - where the Savages were wont to worship and perform sacrifices. The Natives say the spirits still linger there, but we have never seen them."[45]

Native American palisades sometimes contained watchtowers and were often circular or U-shaped. After St. Ignace de Michilimackinac was founded, the French began teaching fort building techniques to the Native Americans. Existing forts were made more defensible by protecting stockades with entrenchments. These later forts would have likely been more rectangular in shape.

The French post, Fort de Buade, is a great mystery. Various dates, names and descriptions can be found. Fort de Buade appears to be a name applied later in the French occupation of St. Ignace. The name Fort Michilimackinac was applied to this location earlier but interchangeably. At times Fort St. Ignace was used. At least one reference exists calling the fort Fort Frontenac.

Descriptions sometimes state that the fort was on the shore. That belief is strongly held by some historians, including some at the Michilimackinac State Park. This theory is supported by a 1744 French map by Jacques Nicholas Bellin. This map shows the "mission detruite" situated north and along the shore from "le fort detruit." Detruite means damaged.

Further support can be found in the detailed descriptions of Cadillac. The last Commandant of Fort de Buade stated, "Opposite the island is a large sandy cove and it is here the French fort is situated… where there is a garrison and the commandant-in-chief of the country resides, who has under him the commandants of various posts; but both he and they are chosen by the governor-general of New France. This post is called Fort de Buade. The Jesuits Mission, the French village and those of the Huron and Odawa are adjacent to one another; and together they border and fill up the head of the cove."[46]

Other descriptions like the two quotes below clearly state the fort was on a hill. In 1938 a congressional appropriation was obtained to rebuild the fort on a hill.

"1673-The year Marquette embarked on his voyage of discovery, the French established a palisade fort at Point St. Ignace. It was situated on an elevation in the rear of the church, facing the bay and was surrounded by a trench and a stockade of cedar pickets. The outlines of the trench are still visible to this day and helped to verify in 1878, the site of the old church and Marquette's grave. That was the first Fort Michilimackinac and must be the one re-garrisoned after the Jesuits burned the church, abandoned the Mission in 1705 and returned to Quebec."[47]

"The former presence of an Indian population on the bluff above that part of St. Ignace popularly known as Vide Poche,[48] is proved by numerous articles of Indian and French manufacture plowed up there by some of the present settlers. The local tradition also places the fort on that height."[49]

Cadillac also left extensive notes in his memoirs regarding the construction of the fort. It was built of three rows of thick stakes. The first row was 30 feet high and was one foot from the second. The third row was 15 feet high and was four feet from the first. The fort was likely surrounded by a dry moat. There were no bastions in the fort.

Commandants reported canoes could not pass without being spotted from the fort. It had an excellent and unobstructed view.

Cadillac later built Fort Detroit (also known as Fort Pontchartrain). No records are known to exist describing the buildings in Fort de Buade; it might be assumed that the make-up would be similar to that found at Fort Detroit. Buildings known to have existed at Fort Detroit included barns, ice houses, trade stores, a church, a public bake house, a windmill used as a flour mill and warehouses which stored the winter food supplies and tons of furs.

Contrary to previous quotes, the date of the initial construction of Fort de Buade is a matter of debate. Opinions vary with some stating it was built in the early 1670s while others state as late as 1690.

No written statement regarding the fort was made upon LaSalle's arrival in the *Griffin* in 1678. Yet Father Louis Hennepin, the Recollet priest who accompanied LaSalle, wrote a detailed description of their visit to Michilimackinac.

Credible accounts state Duluth strengthened the fort or built the fort in 1683 to prepare for a looming attack by the Iroquois. The assumption must be made that some sort of fort existed by 1683. However, in 1683 Duluth held a murder trial at St. Ignace; not at the fort but in the cabin of Sable Odawa Chief Kinonge, the Pike. Why do that if you have a fort? This seems to support the conclusion that the fort was constructed sometime in 1683.

Some historians theorize the fort could not have been built until 1689 based on the way the fort was named. It was named after Louis de Buade de Frontenac. Frontenac had returned to New France to become governor for the second time around that time period. He had served previously from 1672 to 1682, however, weakening the logic behind the theory.

Other evidence supporting theories stating that the fort wasn't built until after 1689 include a map drawn by Louis Armand, Baron de Lahontan which does not show a military fort. Lahontan came to Michilimackinac in 1688 after he visited Fort Niagra and found Commander Chevalier Pierre de Troyes had died. He ordered Fort Niagra burned and the men transferred to Michilimackinac.

Other forts in Michigan in the seventeenth and eighteenth century included Fort Gratiot, Fort Pontchartrain, Fort Miami and a fort built by LaSalle and de Tonty at the mouth of the St. Joseph River in 1679. There were two forts named Fort St. Joseph, one at Niles, Michigan which was built in 1691; and Fort St. Joseph at Port Huron, Michigan which was constructed in 1686 by Duluth. The garrison from Fort St. Joseph at Port Huron, Michigan also relocated to Michilimackinac in 1688 when supplies were found to be inadequate.

Eventually, due to pressure by Cadillac to move the fort to Detroit, Fort de Buade was closed. The closing was immediately recognized as a mistake.

In 1708, the beaver produced from the trade at Michilimackinac was still 50 times greater than that produced from trade at Fort Detroit.[50]

The French sent an official to inspect the posts at Detroit and Michilimackinac. He found Detroit unimpressive and had concerns about Cadillac's rapport with both the Native Americans and the French. He expressed great praise for Michilimackinac, recognizing the advantages of the geography which originally drew the Native Americans to Michilimackinac. He was also impressed with the productivity of corn and the quality of the beaver in the area. The report concluded that if the Huron, lured away to Detroit by Cadillac, were not convinced to return to Michilimackinac they would rejoin the Iroquois out of dissatisfaction with living conditions at Detroit. The inspector suggested Michilimackinac be provided a commandant and a garrison of 30 men.

The Governor General of Canada sent Jesuit Father Joseph Jacques Marest back to St. Ignace and promised to send Louis de la Porte, Sieur de Louvigney, back to St. Ignace to rebuild the fort. Marest requested the government build a fort, houses and send 20 soldiers with a sergeant, in order to impress the Native Americans with their sincerity.

Louvigney returned in 1712. Fort Michilimackinac was rebuilt around 1715, but on the south side of the Straits of Mackinac at what is now called Mackinaw City.

FOOD AND STARVATION

Corn grown at St. Ignace de Michilimackinac drew people looking for supplies. Traders and explorers relied on the Indian corn for their travels, making bread from corn flour dough baked in hot sand or ashes.

Corn or wild rice was mixed with sources of fat, pounded meat or fish, and types of berries and nuts to create pemmican, a primary and highly portable food source. It was pressed into cakes or placed in skin bags and allowed to form a hard ball. It was virtually imperishable. Rose hips or cherries mixed in prevented scurvy. In this way, a bushel of dried corn and 2 pounds of bear grease could feed a person for a month.

Native American women hollowed out logs with fire and placed the hollowed out logs on end. Dried Indian corn was placed in the hollow. A pestle, typically made of wood, was used to pound the corn to a meal. Using this pounded corn, another Native American dish called sagamite was created. The corn meal was boiled in water; fat or fish was added for flavoring. Sagamite was a watery broth-like substance or a mush the consistency of paste.

Native Americans likely also fried or roasted fish using cedar slabs or wrapping the fish in corn husks. Fish were a convenient food source for the nomadic Native American tribes. Fish, especially the whitefish, were considered a staple of the diet. Ample availability of fish was another primary reason for the recognized importance of the Michilimackinac area. Fish were caught with nets on poles, spears through the ice and on bone hooks. The Native Americans speared fish at night using torches of birch bark to attract fish.

Of course, the canoe had great importance to the fisherman. This description relates the use of a fishing canoe in the rapids at Sault Ste. Marie. "The fishing canoe is of small size. It is steered by a man in the stern. The fisherman takes his stand in the bow, sometimes bestriding the light and frail vessel from gunwale to gunwale, having a scoop-net in his hands. This net has a long slender handle, ten feet or more in length. The net is made of strong twine, open at the top, like an entomologist's. When the canoe has been run into the uppermost rapids and a school of fish is seen below or alongside, he dexterously puts down his net and having swooped up a number of the fish, instantly reverses it in water, whips it up and discharges its contents into the canoe. This he repeats till his canoe is loaded, when he shoots out of the tail of the rapids and makes for shore. The fish will average three pounds, but individuals are sometimes two and three times that weight. It is shad-shaped, with well-developed scales, easily removed, but has the mouth of the sucker, very small. The flesh is perfectly white and firm, with very few bones."[51]

Abundant fish may be why the villages at St. Ignace were able to remain intact for 30+ years. Records show that the life spans of Native American villages typically ranged anywhere from 6 to 12 years.[52]

Wild crops collected included: plum, cranberry, pin cherry, blueberry, blackberry, currant, chokecherry, raspberry, rose hip, strawberry, gooseberry, dandelion leave, apple (probably crab apple), acorn, leek, wild rice, honey and maple sugar and syrup. Various species of fish that were harvested included trout, herring, carp, smelt, pickerel, sturgeon (which were 5 to 6 feet long), pike and eel. Birds that were caught and eaten were snipe, partridge, white partridge or ptarmigan, passenger pigeons, geese and turkey. Wild animals that were hunted, trapped or snared for consumption were duck, deer, squirrel, beaver, bear, rabbit, other small mammals and the fat or marrow from larger animals.

"For a decoy they have the skins of Geese, Bustards and Ducks, dry'd and stuffed with hay… In a word, we eat nothing but waterfowl for 15 days."[53]

Foods were preserved by smoking, drying or freezing. Abundant passenger pigeons were harvested with minimal effort. Partially cooked pigeon was preserved by sinking the bird into vessels of bear grease.[54]

Wild rice, found in ponds and on the northern shore of the Straits, was smoked and was another staple of the diet.

Deer and moose were hunted in a manner described in Jesuit Relations as crusting. This type of pursuit took place in the winter after the snow was deep. The snow was required to have a crust thick enough to support hunting dogs and men on snowshoes, but not sufficient to bear the weight of the game.

"The [Native Americans] who spend three parts of four of their lives in hunting in the woods, are very dexterous at that exercise, especially at singling out the trunks of trees upon which the bears nestle... As we were walking up and down in a forest... I heard one savage call to another, 'here's a bear...' For after they'd knocked two or three times upon the trunk of the tree, the bear came out of its hole and was presently shot."[55]

Snares were utilized and snared rabbit was a staple ingredient, used as chicken would be today. Recipes for rabbit or chicken and gleasons, a French dumpling-like noodle, are found in area family recipe files.

Ojibwa and the Huron were known to use hunting fences or to fell trees in a pattern in order to herd animals past waiting hunters.

Torches were installed in the front of canoes that were floated down rivers at night. The deer were hypnotized by the light.

Dog was eaten regularly and considered by some historians to be the Native Americans' only domestic animal, though Cadillac states bear were sometimes tamed.

"The dog among all Indian tribes is more valued and more esteemed than by any people of the civilized world. When they are killed for a feast, it is considered a great compliment and the highest mark of friendship."[56]

Beaver tail, dried buffalo tongue and moose nose were considered delicacies. Snowbirds, also sought after treats, were roasted on a spit.

As early as the 1630s crops were cultivated and shipped from Quebec. These crops included peas, hay, rye, corn, squash, pumpkins, roots and wheat. Quebec had cows and oxen. The area produced and traded lard, butter, oil, cod, several kinds of flour, salt meat, wine, cider, beer and brandy. Supplies of biscuits, bread and hard tack were shipped great distances. There were already established markets and restaurants in Quebec at the time of the founding of St. Ignace. Food shipments were likely not frequent enough to consider the staples anything but a luxury with no potential of completely taking the place of native food sources like fish and wild game.

Salted foods helped habitants get through the long winters but caused scurvy. Spruce sap beer, a Native American remedy, was used to prevent scurvy.

Tea was not available until the early to mid-1700s. Coffee was also not commonly available. The French preferred warmed chocolate, beer or brandy. Teas of wild products were likely consumed including sassafras, Evans or Avens root (also known as Indian Chocolate) and wild mint.

Going to sugar camp in the spring was necessary to survival, but was disguised as a celebration. Those from the Sault area were known to travel to Sugar Island. While in the 1800s, those from Mackinac Island traveled to Bois Blanc Island. Other references state Native American sugar camps were located in the Gros Cap and Cheeseman Road areas, west of St. Ignace. Farther north, the areas of field which now surround Moran were once vast maple forests, supporting Native American sugar camps.

Spiles or taps were made from basswood and pressed into notches in the trees. The sap was collected in birch bark containers with seams sewn of basswood strips. Pitch was used to seal the seams.

Sap was hauled back to camp by human-pulled sleds or by people wearing neck yokes. The sap was too valuable to place in an animal pulled sleigh. A dog team might bolt and spill the cargo. After arriving at a central location in the camp the sap was boiled down over huge fires. Eventually, as the water content in the sap was boiled away candy, sugar and syrups were made.

Maple sugar from the Straits area supplied traders who traveled throughout the entire Great Lakes region. Sugar set aside for trading or later use was buried underground to keep it from souring.

Farming was based on traded information between the Native Americans and the French. At Michilimackinac corn, peas, watermelons, beans and pumpkins were grown. Other domesticated food sources grown by Native Americans in the 1600s included melons, cabbage, onions, radishes, beets, turnips and carrots. The Native Americans also grew tobacco.

Native Americans developed effective ways of clearing land before trade brought metal tools to the Great Lakes. "The easiest way to clear land for crops was to do it like the Indians did, by chopping a deep notch around the base of each tree (girdling). This cut off the sap and caused the tree to die at once. As soon as the leaves fell, the sunshine could get through and the first crops could be planted around the dead trees... Two or three years later the trees would be thoroughly dry and he could burn them down by piling brush around them."[57]

In the early 1670s the Native American population around St. Ignace was estimated at 500, but it soon grew to around 2,000. Due to the concentration of hunters in the area it was necessary to travel great distances from the village to find wild game. Per Baron La Hontan regarding St. Ignace in the 1680s, "The Outaouas (sic) and the Huron could never subsist here, without that fishery; for they are obliged to travel about twenty leagues in the woods before they can kill any harts or elks and it would be infinite fatigue to carry their carcasses so far overland."[58]

Even with the vast menu of foods, starvation was common. Written accounts of starvation were found well into the 1800s. When hunger became unbearable; crow, vulture or anything available would be consumed. Greenish-black, slimy moss called rock tripe was scraped off rocks and known as the fall-back food, eaten in times of extreme starvation. When this was not available moccasins were sometimes consumed. In a few worst case scenarios, victims of hunger resorted to cannibalism. This was taboo in most Native American and European cultures except when it came to the torture of enemies.

LIFE AT
MICHILIMACKINAC

The primary tribes at Michilimackinac were the Odawa, Chippewa and the outnumbered Huron. However, historical references indicate Pottawatomie, Amicouets or the Beaver Nation, Seneca, Illinois, Mohegan, Abenaki, Bone Indians, Menominee, Mohawk and Miami were present at times. Various tribes used the ice bridge and waterway at the Straits as their primary route for migrating from north to south and back.[59] The mix of cultures often caused tension as was expressed by LaSalle. "It is not to be wondered at that the Iroquois speak of waging war against our allies inasmuch as they receive affronts from them every year. I have seen, among the Pottawatomie and Miami at Michilimackinac, the spoils and scalps of numerous Iroquois whom the Indians from this region had treacherously killed while hunting last spring and earlier; which is not unknown to the Iroquois, our allies having the imprudence of celebrating this feat in their presence while they were trading among them, as I have seen Pottawatomie at Michilimack-inac who, dancing with the calumet, boasted of this treachery, holding up the scalps at arms length in the sight of three Mohawk who were there to trade."[60]

Life in Native American villages was shockingly different to European newcomers. Following is an example from Schoolcraft discussing life at Sault Ste. Marie in the 1800s. "I went to rest last night with the heavy murmuring sound of the falls in my ears, broken at short intervals by the busy thump-thump-thump of the Indian drum; for it is to be added, to the otherwise crowded state of the place, that the open grounds and river-side greens of the village, which stretch along irregularly for a mile or two, are filled with the lodges of visiting Indian bands from the interior. The last month of spring and the early summer constitute, in fact, a kind of carnival for the Native Americans. It is at this season that the traders, who have wintered in the interior, come out with their furs to the frontier posts of St. Mary's, Drummond Island and Michilimackinac, to renew their stocks of goods."[61]

Religious beliefs held by Native Americans were not accepted by the Jesuits and often bewildered the French traders and explorers.

"When an inmate of the lodge is sick, to procure a thin sapling some twenty to thirty feet long, from which, after it has been trimmed and the bark is peeled. Native paints are then smeared over it as caprice dictates. To the slender top are then tied bits of scarlet, blue cloth, beads, or some other objects which are deemed acceptable to the Manito or spirit, who has, it is believed, sent sickness to the lodge as a mark of his displeasure. The pole is then raised in front of the lodge and firmly adjusted in the ground. The sight of these Manito poles gives quite a peculiar air to an Indian encampment. Not knowing, however, the value attached to them, one of the officers, a few days after our arrival, having occasion for tent poles, sent one of his men for one of these poles of sacrifice; but its loss was soon observed by the Indians, who promptly reclaimed it and restored it to the exact position which it occupied before."[62]

The Odawa hung stones from piercings in their noses. This ornament which hung down in front of their mouths was meant to protect the wearers from evil spirits. Other adornments, unusual to the Europeans, were noted in the following quote regarding a gathering of Native Americans and French who were preparing to attack the Iroquois. "Had Canada seen such a sight? …Their features were different and so were their manners, their weapons, their decorations and their dances. They sang and whooped and harangued in every accent and tongue. Most of them wore nothing but horns on their heads and the tails of beasts behind their backs. Their faces were painted red or green, with black or white spots; their ears and noses were hung with ornaments of stone; and their naked bodies were daubed with figures of various sorts of animals."[63]

Frequent comments were made by the Jesuits in Jesuit Relations about what they observed. Native Americans were not timid about nakedness. They sacrificed dogs to the Rabbit's Back Peak by tying their feet together and throwing them into the lake. Until the Jesuits tried to end the practice, they sacrificed dogs and tied them to tall Manito poles in the front of their lodges. One of the neighboring Great Lakes tribes, the Illinois, practiced wrapping their dead tribesmen in animal skins and hanging the corpses by the feet and head from tree tops.

"A short time after our arrival we had baptized two twin children, one of whom died a few days later; and, because we had not yet any Cemetery, the relatives suspended this little body in the air, after their usual custom, placing it on a scaffold and then retired into the Forests to pass the winter. A pack of Wolves, pressed with hunger, coming out of the woods, pounced upon this little body; but they, after they had devoured the skins and even the colored glass beads with which it was covered, through a protecting influence that was altogether marvelous, did not touch at all the body itself, as being a thing consecrated by holy Baptism."[64]

While other tribes burned their corpses, used scaffolds or suspended their corpses from trees, at least some of the Odawa practiced burial. An over-sized coffin was built and the body was prepared with the occupant's best garments. Burial of a deceased relative called for the most elegant dress as a matter of family pride. Many tribes believed burial dress became the outfit worn in the afterlife. Into the coffin also went his blanket, gun, ammunition, other weapons, kettle, pipes, mirrors, porcelain collars and death presents.

"Gitche ie nay gow ge ait che gah, 'they have put the sand over him' is a common expression among the Native Americans to indicate that a man is dead and buried. Another mode, delicate and refined in its character, is to suffix the inflection for perfect past tense, 'bun', to a man's name. Thus 'Washington e bun' would indicate that Washington is no more."[65]

Different Native American tribes living at Michilimackinac had different reasons for the way they cared for their deceased. The family of the Great Hare, Odawa which resided at Michilimackinac, believed bodies should be cremated and the ashes thrown into the air. It was believed that failure to do so would prevent the snow from melting, lakes from thawing and spring from coming.

"Indeed, when, a few years ago, the winter had lasted much longer than usual, there was general consternation among... the Great Hare family. They resorted to their customary juggleries; they held several assemblies in order to deliberate upon means of dissipating this unfriendly snow, which was persistently remaining on the ground; when an old woman, approaching them, said: 'My children, you have no sense. You know the commands that the Great Hare left with us, to burn dead bodies and scatter their ashes to the winds, so that they might more quickly return to the Sky, their own country; but you have neglected those commands by leaving, at a few days journey from here, a dead man without burning him, as if he did not belong to the family of the Great Hare. Repair your fault at once' ...Immediately they sent twenty-five men to go to burn this body; about fifteen days were consumed in this journey, during which time the thaw came and the snow disappeared..."[66]

The Huron Tribe's deceased were placed on scaffolds, or at times in graves, but later were reclaimed by family members. The bones were scraped clean and organized into decorated, fur wrapped packets. Eventually, after a great feast, the bone packets were placed in mass graves.

While the Huron treated the bones of their loved ones with a great deal of respect, they were known for harsh treatment of prisoners or those of their own tribe found guilty of murder. The Huron tied murderers to their victim's decaying body and allowed the murderer to starve. *Before the Bridge* describes two skeletons found shackled together during construction on Marquette Street in 1936. Marquette Street is the street on which the Marquette Mission was located. The Huron also employed the firing squad and capital punishment was commonly used on prisoners. Historical accounts state the Huron did not punish tribesmen for theft. They considered artful thieves to be honored and revered. They considered getting caught reason for punishment but not the act itself. When thefts occurred, the French, the Huron and other Native Americans might have been victims.

Envisioning the every day actions of living a Native American life would lead you to picture a village filled with industry. It would take great exertion to maintain enough food for survival.

St. Ignace was described as having fields stretching from the shore inland nine miles. All brush would have been burned to prevent enemies from concealing themselves. This would mean firewood needed to be carried from a distance of ten miles. Areas around the lodges must have stored canoes, firewood supplies and bundles of hides. Drying racks for smoking fish would have prominent places in the villages. Storage areas for nets along the shore would have taken up a great deal of room.

All of the tribes tanned hides; a primary method of doing this involved wiping mashed animal brains on the hide. Skins were smoked, stretched and beaten to preserve and prepare them for clothing and moccasins.

Canoes and snowshoes were manufactured by the Native Americans and traded to the French. They sold sheets of bark for cabins and canoes. They also traded strawberries, blueberries, other fruits and maple sugar.

In the nomadic and migratory lifestyle of the Native Americans, the onset of sugaring season brought them back from their winter hunting camps to sugar camp. The end of sugar season signaled time to return to the Straits to trade, back to where the Jesuits could continue their teachings. Though great efforts were undertaken by the Jesuits to impress French values on the Native Americans; it soon became apparent the French coureur de bois were absorbing Native American customs at a much quicker pace. Many had found trade advantages in marrying in the manner of the country and lived in the traditions of their Native American in-laws. Some took wives in the country and in Montreal or Quebec, using aliases to hide indiscretions. Historic writings refer to them as having taken to the woods or having gone native, using grease as protection from insects and vermilion to paint their faces red in the Native American way.

The region was still more Native American in character than French when LaSalle, de Tonty and Hennepin arrived on the *Griffin* in 1678.

The *Griffin* anchored in East Moran bay overlooking Rabbit's Back Peak, "…she found her rest behind the point of St. Ignace of Michilimackinac, floating in that tranquil cove where crystal waters cover but cannot hide the pebbly depths beneath. Before her rose the house and chapel of the Jesuits, enclosed with palisades; on the right, the Huron village, with its bark cabins and its fence of tall pickets; on the left, the square compact houses of the French traders; and, not far off, the clustered wigwams of an Odawa village. Here was the center of the Jesuit missions and a center of the Indian trade… Keen traders, with or without a license; and lawless coureurs de bois, whom a few years of forest life had weaned from civilization, made St. Ignace their resort; and here there were many of them when the *Griffin* came."[67]

LaSalle's party heard mass at a chapel in the Odawa village and then set about retrieving trade goods stolen by lawless employees. "His own followers, too, had been tampered with. In the autumn before, it may be remembered, he had sent fifteen men up the lakes, to trade for him, with orders to go thence to the Illinois and make preparation against his coming. Early in the summer, de Tonty had been dispatched in a canoe, from Niagara, to look after them… Most of the men had been seduced from their duty and had disobeyed their orders, squandered the goods entrusted to them, or used them in trading on their own account. LaSalle found four of them at Michilimackinac. These he arrested and sent de Tonty to the Falls of Ste. Marie, where two others were captured, with their plunder. The rest were in the woods and it was useless to pursue them."[68]

Henri de Tonty who was LaSalle's trusted second in command was the older brother of Alphonse de Tonty, who was Cadillac's second in command. Alphonse de Tonty later became Commandant of Fort Pontchartrain in Detroit and Michilimackinac. Both de Tontys (sometimes spelled Tonti) appear throughout the early history of St. Ignace de Michilimackinac.

Henri de Tonty returned to Michilimackinac again and again over a 20-year period. As was previously stated, he was with LaSalle at Michilimackinac in 1678. In 1681, Henri de Tonty returned to Michilimackinac to recover after being stabbed by an Iroquois (Onondaga) at Fort Creve Coeur, near what is now Peoria, Illinois. He was still using Michilimackinac as a base of operations when Cadillac was appointed commander of the post in 1694.

By the 1700s de Tonty's knowledge of the colony had earned him a great deal of respect. His letters were provided directly to the King. The King made decisions regarding the governing of the colony directly based on Henri de Tonty's advice. De Tonty had been assigned to a post at Mobile, Alabama by 1704 where he died from yellow fever.

Younger brother, Alphonse de Tonty, was most likely with Cadillac during the initial planning for the founding of Detroit. This planning took place at Michilimackinac.

At the time of his recall from Fort de Buade in 1696, Cadillac was forming a plan to build a fort and settlement at a narrowing in the Detroit River. His motivations included protecting the trade from the British colonists, securing a buffer against the Iroquois, relocating to a better climate for personal reasons and growing better crops. He sought to have the Native Americans from Michilimackinac settle at the post in Detroit.

During this same time, Father Etienne Carheil was lobbying the government to remove the Fort de Buade garrison. He wished to curb the increasing corruption present at Michilimackinac by reducing the influence of Cadillac and the soldiers. But the plan backfired and in a short time many of the Native Americans had been coaxed to Detroit. Soon after, Carheil and Jesuit Joseph Jacques Marest gave up and burned the chapel to the ground.

It appears Cadillac and de Tonty were originally close. Cadillac's wife, Marie Therese Guyon and de Tonty's wife, Marie-Anne Picot Belestre, traveled through the wilderness together, arriving first at Detroit in 1702, making them arguably the first European women to live in Michigan.

Cadillac and Alphonse de Tonty returned to Michilimackinac to fetch 198 pots of brandy hidden near St. Ignace. They also retrieved a cannon, some muskets and ammunition. The lawlessness of Michilimackinac followed Cadillac to Fort Detroit; one of Cadillac's jobs at Fort Detroit was to vigilantly check canoes for brandy.

Eventually, Cadillac's trust for de Tonty waned. He became suspicious that Alphonse de Tonty had joined with the Jesuits from Michilimackinac, supporting a plan to build a new post on Lake Michigan. De Tonty admitted his responsibility and Cadillac forgave the lack of loyalty.

Soon suspicions turned against Cadillac. In 1704 an investigation of Cadillac was begun by the Company of the Colony, the governing French conglomerate that controlled the fur trade at the time. Cadillac arrested the investigator but soon found the tables turned. He was arrested in Quebec upon his return. De Tonty was left in charge of the garrison and settlement until Cadillac was released.

Cadillac continued to doubt de Tonty and determined that he had been involved in illegal fur trade, using assets of the Company of the Colony for trade. Cadillac's accusations turned against him. A relative of the governor-general was involved with de Tonty. A counter complaint was lodged and Cadillac again found himself in trouble. He was soon acquitted but Cadillac was temporarily forbidden from returning to Detroit.

Traders

The term coureur de bois (coureurs de bois, plural) was used as early as 1615 to denote travelers to the undeveloped, inland areas of New France. Later the term was applied to illegal traders, specifically those trading without proper permits and permissions. Synonyms for the term include woods runner, bush ranger and bush loper. They were often described as hard living, unrestrained, untamed outlaws. They were equally adapted to life on the water or as hunters in the woods.

Coureur de bois traveled mostly in groups of three. They carried tarps for shelter or to use as sails. Free time was spent smoking, drinking, singing songs, gambling and seducing women.

If caught, coureurs de bois were threatened with branding, beatings, fines, imprisonment in Mediterranean galleys or even forcible employment as rowers for politician's canoes. However, evidence shows the people of the colony, including the judges and government officials, conspired to protect this way of life and most often looked the other way. Most offenders, if punished, were given fines and then returned to lives of freedom and trading.

Voyageurs, as opposed to coureurs de bois, traded with licenses or were away from the populated areas of New France with government permission. There were many more coureurs de bois than voyageurs.

Both legal and illegal trading continued throughout the entire history of New France and into the 1800s. Estimates for the number of illegal traders grew until an estimated 40% of the male French population in the 1670s and 1680s were labeled coureur de bois.

Beaver pelts were New France's most valuable currency. They were shipped to Europe to make beaver felt hats which were so valuable they were willed from father to son. A hunter seeking beaver was expected to harvest 50 or 60 per month during the winter. The pelts were traded and graded according to the quality of the pelt and the skill of the hide preparation.

Less common furs traded included otter, mink, buffalo, marten, swan skin and ermine. Silver fox commanded a premium. Traders in North America also harvested and traded whalebone, ivory, elk hooves and whale blubber.

Skins, not money, acted as currency and remained so for more than 150 years through the French, British and American regimes. If a price was applied to a piece of merchandise it was applied in skins. Rewards were paid by the government in skins. In the northern Great Lakes beaver was the standard. In the southern Great Lakes raccoon skins were the standard.

Trade items included mirrors, buttons, awls, knives, needles, scrapers, glass beads, hatchets, metal arrow heads, files, kettles, tobacco, cloth, blankets, ribbons, flints and strikers, tacks, hinges, latches, nails, jewelry, shoes, musket balls, powder, tools, rope, red flannel, brandy, traps, vermilion and guns. At one point in the fur trade, 15,000 gallons of liquor was traded at Michilimackinac annually. Slaves were also traded.

In 1685 according to Jesuit Pierre-François-Xavier de Charlevoix, three quarters of the fur being shipped East was coming from the Great Lakes Native American tribes. By the end of the 1600s local fur supplies were dwindling. Fur traders moved westward seeking new supplies.

Bombarded by complaints from the Jesuits of debauchery and evil influences on the Native Americans, fur trade in the Great Lakes was completely banned by King Louis the XIV in 1696. This was one of many times that trade was made illegal throughout the history of New France. All French persons were ordered to return East, regardless of infirmity or reason, under threat of confinement in the Mediterranean galleys. However, many French were married into the fur trade and refused to abandon their country wives and children. After many decades of French intermarriage with the Native American population, control of the fur trade became impossible.

The ban did not include trading with the Dakota and other western tribes. This caused the trade dependent Native Americans at Michilimackinac and Green Bay to conspire to be rid of the French.

About this same time there was a downturn in the fur trade due to a ten year of overstock of beaver pelts. This gave Cadillac an opening to encourage the French King to close

Fort de Buade. He wished to move the garrison and as many Native Americans as would accompany him to Fort Pontchartrain (Fort Detroit).

The Jesuits attempted to prevent the Native American population from following Cadillac. In return Cadillac put forth great effort to undermine the Jesuits. He referred to the priests as obstinate and accused them of conspiracy. He referred to the Jesuits as subversive and was particularly hostile toward Jesuit Etienne Carheil, who had written many complaint letters to the government against Cadillac. Carheil accused Cadillac of encouraging the Native Americans' alcohol consumption and misbehavior.

Cadillac did encourage alcohol consumption and strongly stated that brandy was a necessity of the fur trade. He was also of the opinion that mixed marriages were a necessity and did little to separate the French men and Native American women, stating, "Many of the Indian girls do live vicious lives, but that is because the teachers are too strict with them and try to make them nuns. Much better let them marry our soldiers and then educate their children."[69]

Native trade relationships and ownership of trade routes were family based. An advantageous marriage could mean huge profit, trade opportunity and trapping territory. Many marriages were arranged, keeping such commerce in mind. Some French excused polygamy as a commercial necessity.

The French were losing hold of the fur trade by the 1700s. The coureurs de bois were turning to the Hudson's Bay Company, an English syndicate begun by disgruntled French traders Grossiellers and Radisson.

Constant Marchand Sieur de Lignery was sent to Michilimackinac to offer the coureurs de bois yet another amnesty in 1713. Amnesty for coureurs de bois was offered and retracted on many occasions. King Louis XIV decreed forgiveness to the "woods runners" and clemency from prosecution.

"Why think you could license and keep in order bushrangers? You had to catch you bush runner first."[70]

In 1715, after 19 years, the 1696 ban on trading was abandoned. Finally, those remaining illegal traders were made legal once again. Shortly afterward King Louis the XIV died.

WAR AND MIGRATION

The Odawa and the Huron lived east of and were also scattered throughout the islands of Lake Huron in the 1400s and 1500s. The Chippewa and Pottawatomie were living near and around the Straits of Mackinac.

At the time of the arrival of Father Marquette, the area Native Americans were decades deep into the bloody Beaver Wars (1630-1700) against the Iroquois Nations. These wars drove the Mackinac area tribes from east to west, further west and then back to Mackinac again.

Iroquois occupied the St. Ignace area around 1630; Odawa and Chippewa occupied the Gros Cap area.

Life at Michilimackinac was not peaceful. As the Jesuits recorded Native American oral history they learned that generations before, perhaps around 1630, a battle had taken place on the point of land currently known as Graham's Point. The battle is discussed in the book *Before the Bridge*. "At one time a group of Iroquois settled on the shore facing the Straits, which gave rise to the name, Iroquois Point (now Graham's Point). They were wiped out in a massacre by the Indians settled at Gros Cap, under Chief Saugeman... Only some of the women and children survived the massacre."[71]

Thereafter, the name assigned to that point was the Point of the Iroquois Woman or Iroquois Point. Graham's Point is the point of land most southerly and easterly in the City of St. Ignace. This point of land, which protrudes toward Mackinac Island, is visible from the right side of the Mackinac Bridge when headed north toward the tollbooths.

Jean Nicholet, one of the first documented explorers to see Lake Michigan, met to trade with Odawa and Huron in 1634. They were located near Green Bay, Wisconsin. The area was also occupied by Winnebago. The Winnebago were displeased by the loss in territory resulting from the westward movement of the Odawa, Chippewa and Huron. The Winnebago took out their aggression on the Odawa. The Odawa sent emissaries to try peace negotiations but the emissaries were killed and eaten by the Winnebago. Nicholet helped negotiate a lasting peace that allowed the Odawa and the Huron more movement around the Great Lakes. The Odawa moved to Michilimackinac around 1640.

Movement of the Odawa toward Mackinac resulted in territorial wars with the Bone or Assegun Indians in the 1640s. Assegun Indians lived on the southern shore of the Upper Peninsula near what is now St. Ignace and north. The Odawa joined with the Chippewa and a great battle took place near DeTour, Michigan. This resulted in the Assegun retreating to a position near what is now Mackinaw City, Michigan. The Assegun built a village in this location but continued to launch raids on the nearby Odawa villages. The Odawa eventually drove the raiders from the country, south to the Grand Rapids area where the remaining Assegun were assimilated into the Mascouten Tribe. Historians believe earthworks in the St. Ignace area and west are the work of the Bone Indians.

About this same time the Chippewa defeated and absorbed the Mundua, who had occupied the Northern Lower Peninsula.

Odawa were still, or again, in the Straits area in 1649. At the same time the Huron, who were living east of Lake Huron, fled the Iroquois. Eventually, Iroquois guns and European disease reduced the number of the Huron to 1,000. Being reduced in number meant being drastically prone to further attacks. The Huron relocated to Michilimackinac where they found the Odawa, and for part of the year they found the Ojibwa. From 1650 to 1685 Jesuit Relations states, "the Saulter (Chippewa) inhabited the Straits area seasonally in the winter when the fish were less plentiful in Sault Ste. Marie."[72] The combined Mackinac area tribes were attacked by the Iroquois in 1650 but they succeeded in fending them off. A year later the Huron and Odawa moved further west to Green Bay, Wisconsin in order to avoid the Iroquois. The relocated tribes at Green Bay were tracked down by 800 Iroquois who assaulted a combined force of Odawa, Huron and Pottawatomie in 1653 at Mitchigami, on the Door Peninsula, Wisconsin. The combined force waited out the Iroquois attack in a fortified village. The Iroquois assault failed and on returning to their villages the Iroquois were attacked by Ojibwa warriors. Half of the Iroquois force were killed by the Ojibwa.

During this time period the fur trade was controlled by the Iroquois. They had blocked the Ottawa River, the passage from the Great Lakes to Montreal.

Also during 1658 the Sturgeon Wars pitted the Ojibwa against the Menominee in Wisconsin. The battling began when the Menominee built fish weirs on the Menominee

River, blocking the movement of fish toward Ojibwa villages. The actual underlying cause may have been the mix and diversity of population in the general Green Bay area. Many tribes including the Ojibwa, Pottawatomie, Huron, Odawa, Fox, Menominee and Noquet lived in the area and joined in the skirmishes.

Huron moved to the Lake Pepin area on the Mississippi River between Wisconsin and Minnesota in 1658. The Odawa relocated to join the Chippewa on the Keweenaw Peninsula and the south and west shores of Lake Superior.

The Iroquois planned another attack against the Odawa and Huron camps on the south shore of Lake Superior in 1662. The Iroquois never made it through Chippewa territory. A party of Ojibwa, Huron and Odawa surprised an unaware war party of 100 Mohawk and Oneida warriors on the shores of Lake Superior, at what is now called Iroquois Point near Brimley, Michigan. A massive defeat followed with few survivors on the Iroquois side.

Historians also note that sometime prior to 1665, prior to the arrival of the Jesuits, a battle took place in the valley behind what is now the Gros Cap cemetery.

Odawa, Ojibwa, Huron, Fox, Sauk, some Potawatami and the Kickapoo were in Wisconsin by 1665. This resulted in tensions between these tribes and the Dakota developing by the late 1660s.

In the spring of 1671 the Huron, accompanied by Father Marquette, returned to Michilimackinac from villages on Lake Superior. They soon joined the Odawa of Manitoulin Island, the Pottawatomie, Fox and Sauk on the warpath. The total warriors numbered 1,000. They traveled through Wisconsin, attacking the Dakota with great casualties. The defeated war party retreated back to Michigan as winter descended and starvation ensued. The Huron warriors covered the rear of the retreating war party. By 1673 Marquette reported the Huron population had been reduced to 380.

War continued between the Dakota and the Ojibwa until 1680 when Daniel Greysolon Duluth negotiated peace between the warring tribes.

Possibly advantaged by the absence of those in the war party fighting the Dakota, the Seneca (Iroquois) attacked and burned the mission and villages at St. Ignace in 1671. The Huron neared extinction and their Algonquin neighbors, the Odawa, were greatly reduced by the time of their return in 1673. Decreased population continued to make St. Ignace vulnerable to the Iroquois.

In the mid 1670s the Senecas sent ambassadors with gifts to the Huron, attempting to induce them to join in attacking the Dakota. This temporary peace with the Seneca eventually led to disaster. In 1682 a Seneca chief named Annanhaa was killed by the Illinois while visiting the Odawa village at Gros Cap after he refused to give up an Illinois child he kept as a slave. The Beaver Wars flared again and the Michilimackinac tribes were caught in the middle.

The Michilimackinac tribes sought French protection. But Huron Chief Kondiaronk had different plans. Behind the backs of the Algonquins and the French he made peaceful overtures to the Iroquois, leaving the Odawa and Chippewa to fend for themselves. These actions spurred mistrust between the Michilimackinac tribes. Meanwhile, the Iroquois continued to obliterate Native American Nations lying in the southern and western Great Lakes area.

Most of the warfare between 1680 and 1683 took place in the Illinois villages near southern Lake Michigan. By 1683 violence had returned to Michilimackinac. The Frenchman in charge of the garrison was former bodyguard to the King, Daniel Greysolon Duluth. The French led by Duluth, fortified and prepared the fort for a possible attack. Orders were sent to outlying posts for the French and Native Americans to return to Mackinac. The Seneca attacked the Odawa villages near St. Ignace again in 1683.

The Illinois had been severely punished and virtually obliterated by the Seneca by 1684. The Seneca were bathing in glory and with maximum confidence, attacked Fort St. Louis. This expedition failed and was a turning point in the Beaver Wars.

By 1687 New France was facing famine and the fur trade faced ruin. New Governor of Canada, Jacques-Rene de Brisay de Denonville, resolved to control the Iroquois and the fur trade in Canada. He set goals of strengthening forts, building new forts and he finally saw the advantage of providing the Great Lakes tribes with guns. Prior, the French had withheld guns from their allies, the Algonquins, while the English and Dutch had supplied the Iroquois Nations with guns. The French again attempted to negotiate peace.

Huron Chief Kondiaronk was determined to defeat the efforts toward peace. He learned of peace talks and captured peace delegates sent by the Iroquois to meet with French officials. He killed an Iroquois chief and then deviously told the

Iroquois prisoners that the French had tricked him into attacking them. He then released all the prisoners except one which he handed over to the French Commandant at Michilimackinac, slyly suggesting the Commandant execute the remaining prisoner. The commandant, uninformed of the attempts at peace, put the prisoner in front of a firing squad.

It was not the end of Kondiaronk's deception. Kondiaronk then released an Iroquois slave who resided in the village, allowing him to return to his tribe with the news of the French execution; thus, completing the deception and ending all chances at peace.

Kondiaronk had completely changed his strategy and had a new goal by 1689. He joined with the Iroquois to destroy his neighbors, the Odawa.

The new French policies had begun to work by the 1690s. The Michilimackinac tribes including the Huron, Chippewa and Odawa began to move eastward. They again occupied the areas east of Lake Huron and the Lake Huron islands. Old disputes between the Fox and the Chippewa resulted in skirmishes between the two Algonquin tribes. However, the relative peace in the region still allowed trade to flourish. This turned out to have negative consequences. By the late 1690s, fur was overstocked and prices began to plummet. Complaints about the morals of lawless and licentious traders reached France. Louis XIV closed the fur trade on the Great Lakes in 1696.

By 1697 the Michilimackinac Huron had split into two groups. One followed Kondiaronk to side with the French. The other followed Huron Chief Le Baron, siding with the English. These groups feuded and when Le Baron's warriors planned an attack on the Miami with the help of the Iroquois, Koniaronk warned the Miami. He then attacked a party of Iroquois on Lake Erie, killing many and preventing Le Baron's group from allying with the Iroquois.

The Algonquin tribes agreed to peace with the Iroquois in 1701. The Beaver Wars were officially over. Ironically, Huron Chief Kondiaronk died while attending the peace talks.

ENGLISH PLAN ATTACKS ON MICHILIMACKINAC

By the end of the seventeenth century, English from New England colonies and Dutch from New York had developed designs on Mackinac trade.

Governor Dongan of New York issued a trade license to Canadian LaFontaine Marion to trade in the upper Great Lakes in 1685. The trip caused Canadian Governor Denonville great concern. Denonville realized English trade practices greatly favored the Native Americans.

English traders reached Michilimackinac in 1686, where they traded furs freely. The French garrison did not interfere. The commandant of Fort de Buade, De la Durantaye, was gone and returned just after the English trade party left. Within a year, two more English trading expeditions had left Albany with cargos of rum. The parties laid up with the Seneca for the winter, heading for Michilimackinac in the spring of 1687.

Denonville had planned attacks against the Iroquois and had sent word to French posts around the Great Lakes to rendezvous at Niagara. Duluth, De Tonty and Francois de La Forest were commanding surrounding posts. Durantaye, then commander of Fort de Buade, came upon and captured the first English party 60 miles short of reaching Michilimackinac and took prisoners. He then joined up with Duluth, De Tonty and La Forest below Fort St. Joseph on Lake Erie. They proceeded to Niagara, capturing the second party on the way.

The English and Dutch were taken prisoners and transported to Michilimackinac. A French deserter, acting as an interpreter and guide, was put to death on the spot. The goods they carried were disseminated among the allied Native Americans.

Though such feats seem to evidence French strength, the Native Americans were beginning to doubt the ability of the French to protect them against the Iroquois. In 1688 the Iroquois successfully attacked Montreal, leading the Odawa to explore peace with the English. The Iroquois applied pressure by offering to cease hostilities if the Huron and Odawa would renounce the French King and join with the English.

Meanwhile, Father Etienne Carheil was trying to warn Governor Frontenac that the Native Americans at Michilimackinac were waning. Carheil goaded French officials, calling them apathetic, attempting to prod them into action. He feared the Huron and Odawas were about to turn to the receptive alliance between the English, Iroquois and Dutch. The alliance offered assurance of their safety from the Iroquois and would allow them to take advantage of greater trading profits. He warned of the great monetary losses.

Encouraged by the Native Americans in the region, 70 Englishmen planned to capture Michilimackinac in 1689. The English intended to seize all furs stored at Michilimackinac as retribution for the losses experienced in their 1687 expedition. The Governor of Montreal learned of the plot in advance and thwarted the attack.

Seventy years later, the English succeeded in exacting their revenge and won the territory in the French and Indian War. The area Native American tribes steadfastly supported the French.

Travel

U ntil long after the building of the *Griffin*, canoes were the primary source of transportation on the Great Lakes. The typical canoe used for long trips was 35 to 40 feet long and was called a batteaux. A batteaux could carry many tons of trade items and fur. Passengers settled on bundles of fur or whatever freight was contained within the wooden ribs. The boats were constructed without seats. Smaller, lighter canoes were used for fishing.

Travelers by canoe hugged the shores of the Great Lakes for safety, avoiding open water. They did not travel through the inland areas to any great extent.

Henry Schoolcraft, Government Indian Agent is Sault Ste. Marie, Michigan in the early 1800s, traveled by canoe often. He wrote that he canoed from Sault Ste. Marie to Michilimackinac, 90 miles, in an overnight trip. Once he made the trip to and back twice, 360 miles, within a 6-day time span. In other text he discussed traveling approximately 70 miles in one day. The speed varied with the weather and water current. Historians and mapmakers estimated canoes could travel 45 miles or 15 leagues per day downstream and half that going upstream. Informally, distance was measured by the Native Americans and French in pipes smoked.

"Nijopwagan" meant two pipes which was approximately an hour.

Life revolved around the water because there were no roads. Every distance and landmark described in that time period was based on observation from the water.

There were no roads, no road signs and few maps. Lower limbs were removed from conifer trees to signal portages or other significant points on the water trail.

In the winter snowshoes or "racquettes" were the primary source of transportation. Dog trains, toboggans and Creole sleighs were also noted as transportation by Schoolcraft.

"When I first put these great flat skates on my feet, I thought that I should fall with my nose in the snow, at every step I took. But experience has taught me that God provides for the convenience of all nations according to their needs. I walk very freely now on these raquettes. As to the [Native Americans] they do not hinder them from jumping like bucks or running like deer."[73]

Author's Note: Similes like the one above comparing Native Americans to animals are constantly found in research from the time period. The research is fraught with statements containing stereo-typing and inappropriate labeling (savage, infidel). Some historians wonder if statements like these may be a window into the prejudices harbored by some of the missionaries and other Europeans. One has to wonder, as did many of the French at the time, as to the true motivations of some who claimed to help or save the souls of the Native American people.

Slaves and Captives

The earliest exploration of New France was driven by European slave traders. As early as the year 1500, Native Americans were being sold by the Portuguese in Europe. King Henri VII had three Native American slaves by 1502.

Ships arrived in New France seeking adventure, fish and furs. Vacant cargo areas were filled with slaves. Slave trader Thomas Aubert was credited with discovering Quebec.

Slavery was legal in New France until 1834, decades after Canada was lost to the English. Thousands of African slaves were brought to New France by the habitants. Thousands more were Native American slaves called Panis, a derivative of the word Pawnee. They were owned by both the French and other Native Americans. Pawnee is the name of a Plains tribe from which many slaves were captured. The use of the label Panis did not necessarily mean the slave was of the Pawnee Tribe.

The Church was identified by some as the largest slaveholder in New France. Child slaves worked in the missions and houses of charity for both the Ursuline Mothers and the Jesuits.

Some historians believe that by demanding children to be used as slaves in the missions, the Jesuits instigated raiding and war. The explorers and Jesuits at Michilimackinac were no exception. Marquette was given a little boy as a slave by the Illinois while searching for the Mississippi with Joliet.

"When I had finished my speech, the sachem rose and laying his hand on the head of a little slave, whom he was about to give us, spoke thus: 'I thank thee, Blackgown and thee, Frenchman,' addressing M. Jollyet, 'for taking so much pains to come and visit us. Never has the earth been so beautiful, nor the sun so bright, as to-day. Never has our river been so calm, nor so free from rocks, which your canoes have removed as they passed. Never has our tobacco had so fine a flavor, nor our corn appeared so beautiful as we behold it to-day. Here is my son, that I give thee, that thou mayst know my heart. I pray thee to take pity on me and all my nation. Thou knowest the Great Spirit who has made us all. Thou speakest to him and hearest his word: ask him to give me life and health and come and dwell with us, that we may know him.' Saying this, he placed the little slave near us and made us a second present, an all-mysterious calumet, which they value more than a slave."[74]

Many marriages took place between French colonists and African and Native American slaves. More often than not the slaves continued to be enslaved. The situation commonly led to offspring being fathered by the slave owners. In 1695 a law was enacted by the King of France fining men 2,000 pounds of sugar if convicted of fathering a child with a slave. It was rarely enforced as this had become culturally acceptable.

Slave owners felt no apprehension about separating the children of the slaves from their mothers, even when the offspring might be their own child. The child of a slave was specifically defined as a slave until the 1720s.

Slaves and children of slaves often took the last name of their owners.

Punishment for slaves attempting to escape included branding the slave with a hot iron, cutting off their ears, cutting the slave's hamstrings or death.

Such brutal acts were not reserved for slaves only. There are many instances of brutal, inhumane treatment of prisoners by both the French and Native American tribes. There are many recorded occasions where prisoners, often Seneca or other Iroquois, were taken to Michilimackinac. In 1688 records indicate a French firing squad was used to put a prisoner to death at Michilimackinac. More often, when prisoners were put to death they were burned alive. In accordance with beliefs held by many different Native American tribes, the prisoners were sometimes cooked and eaten.

In the letter below, in August of 1695 from Fort de Baude, Cadillac bragged about how viciously prisoners were treated.

"As there was a cessation of hostilities, on propositions of peace made by the Iroquois, which much apparent submission, it was necessary to make great efforts to induce all these nations to recommence the war, according to the orders I had received. Although there went out from here and from the villages depending upon this post, about eight or nine hundred men, in different parties, they only brought in fifty-six scalps and made four prisoners, whom we burned, according to their custom, notwithstanding all the assurances the victims could give that a treaty of peace had already been made at Montreal.

As the Iroquois are not to be trusted, our allies were not disposed to believe the assurances of the prisoners and finally subjected them to the usual treatment of those who fall alive into the hands of their enemies. There are several parties which have not yet returned; if they bring any prisoners to me, I can assure you their fate will be no sweeter than that of the others…"[75]

BRANDY AND VICES

The use of alcoholic spirits in the fur trade was a matter of great debate. In 1678 LaSalle, Joliet and various other men who frequented Michilimackinac participated in the Brandy Parliament. It was a meeting of the most powerful traders, explorers, merchants, religious icons and government officials in New France. The objective of the meeting was to determine a policy to be presented to the King and enforced as law regarding the use of liquor in the fur trade.

Some attending the meeting argued against providing liquor to the Native Americans, pointing out that time spent drinking meant less time hunting and trapping. LaSalle led the debate to continue trading with liquor, assuming liquor would just be smuggled West anyway and the Natives would simply turn to the illegal sources, or worse, the English.

Joliet, who was educated by the Jesuits, advocated 100% prohibition. He supported his position by pointing to erosion of Native American family life, less time spent hunting and increased indebtedness. He commented that situations at times became uncontrollably violent. Joliet advocated putting to death any trader caught providing the Native Americans with brandy.

In the end the Parliament voted to continue to allow traders to use liquor in the fur trade. The debate did not end, however, in 1694 the French King forbid traders at Michilimackinac from using alcohol in trade which created a one town prohibition. In the following letter, written in August of 1695, Cadillac voiced his opinion of the prohibition.

Monsieur:

You already know, without doubt, that Count Frontenac appointed me, last year to the command of this country, in the place of M. Louvigny…

In regard to the decision made by the court, concerning the transportation of liquors to this place, I am far from daring to disapprove of it; but nothing can induce me to be entirely silent on a subject involving so deeply the interest of the king.

It is a great mistake, if people have an idea that this place is deserted, this village is one of the largest in all Canada. There is a fine fort of pickets and sixty houses, that form a street in a straight line. There is a garrison of well-disciplined, chosen soldiers, consisting of about two hundred men, the best-formed and most athletic to be found in this New World; besides many other persons who are residents here during two or three months in the year. This being an indubitable fact, it seems to me that this place should not be deprived of the privilege which His Majesty has accorded to all the other places and villages in Canada - the privilege of furnishing themselves with the necessary drinks for their use. If there are but few places which should enjoy this liberty, this would undoubtedly be one, as it is exposed to all kinds of fatigue. The situation of the place and the food, also, require it.

BRANDY AND VICES

The houses are arranged along the shore of this great Lake Huron and fish and smoked meat constitute the principal food of the inhabitants, so that a drink of brandy, after the repast, seems necessary to cook the bilious meats and the crudities which they leave in the stomach. The air is penetrating and corrosive and without the brandy that they use in the morning, sickness would be much more frequent.

The villages of the Savages, in which there are six or seven thousand souls, are about a pistol-shot distant from ours. All the lands are cleared for about three leagues around their village and perfectly well cultivated. They produce a sufficient quantity of Indian corn for the use of both the French and savage inhabitants. The question is, then, what reason can there be for this prohibition of intoxicating drinks, in regard to the French who are here now and who only go and come once a year? Are they not subjects of the king, even as others? In what country, then, or in what land, until now, have they taken from the French the right to use brandy, provided they did not become disorderly?

Now what reason can one assign that the Savages should not drink brandy bought with their own money as well as we? Is it prohibited to prevent them from becoming intoxicated? Or is it because the use of brandy reduces them to extreme misery - placing it out of their power to make war, by depriving them of clothing and arms?... The law strictly forbids any one to trade with the Savages for their arms, under pain of a large pecuniary fine. As for their clothing, can any one assert that clothing is necessary for them when they go to war, since everybody knows that it is the custom of all nations here, when they go to eat their enemy on his own land, they go naked... It is bad faith to represent to the County that the sale of brandy reduces the savage to a state of nudity and by that means places it out of his power to make war; since he never goes to war in any other condition.

...Perhaps it will be said that the sale of brandy makes the labors of the missionaries unfruitful... If it is the use of brandy that hinders the advancement of the cause of God, I deny it; for it is a fact which no one can deny, that there are a great number among the Savages who never drink brandy, yet who are not, for that, better Christians.[76]

There was a great deal of profit to be made from bringing liquor to Michilimackinac, where it sold for more than eight times cost. Cadillac was thought to not only support the use of alcohol but engage in the sale of liquor. On his way to build Detroit he went out of his way to St. Ignace. "Cadillac took a quick trip up to Mackinac. He found four hundred barrels of unlicensed brandy bought at three dollars a pot and sold at twenty to twenty-five dollars to Natives and when he came back to seize it in 1701, he found left only one hundred and ninety-eight pots; so one may infer it was not his brandy. Mackinac was simply a haunt of uncontrolled crime."[77]

Father Etienne de Carheil was on to Cadillac and wrote scathing letters criticizing Cadillac's leadership and those who served under him. In letters he and others accused Cadillac of being evil, brutal, violent, unjust, lewd, shameless, contemptuous and insulting. He complained of open and unrestrained trade in brandy and complained that they would have to abandon the mission to habitually and universally drunk and immoral brandy traders. The Church declared trade in brandy a mortal sin.

"...the infamous and baleful trade of brandy gives rise everywhere without restraint. In our despair there is no other step to take than to leave our missions and abandon them to the brandy traders, so that they may establish their trade of drunkenness and immortality."[78]

The Jesuits also disapproved of the French treatment and interaction with Native American women. The following is an excerpt from a letter written by Denonville, discussing the position of persons against providing alcohol to the Native Americans and illustrating how the French were using the Native American women.

"In spite of the king's edicts, the coureurs de bois have carried a hundred barrels of brandy to Michilimackinac in a single year; and their libertinism and debauchery have gone to such an extremity that it is a wonder the Indians have not massacred them all to save themselves from their violence and recover their wives and daughters from them."[79]

Carheil specifically spoke of the French luring the women to their houses under false pretenses. The Frenchmen claimed to need help around the house pounding corn, chopping wood, cooking or making shoes, but were accused of hoping to purchase other services. Traders were known to take prostitutes on trading journeys.

"...making of their fort a place that I am ashamed to call by its proper name, where the women have found out that their bodies might serve in lieu of merchandise and would be still better received than beaver-skins. All the soldiers keep open house in their dwellings for all the women of their acquaintance. From morning to night, they pass entire days there, one after another, sitting by their fire and often on their beds, engaged in conversations and actions proper to their commerce. This generally ends only at night, because the crowd is too great during the day to allow of their concluding it then, although they frequently arrange among themselves to leave a house empty, so as not to defer the conclusion until night."[80]

The French kept public taverns, gambled for whole days and nights and fought until at times gunfire broke out. The Native Americans joined in the action, gambling and drinking. On an occasion that a French dignitary visited, a band of Odawa consumed five casks of brandy. Becoming extremely intoxicated they set fire to their own wigwams and jeered the French when they put out the fires.

"So much is this the case that all the villages of our Savages are now only Taverns, as regards drunkenness; and sodoms, as regards immorality from which we must withdraw and which we must abandon to the just anger and vengeance of God."[81]

Ultimately, the Jesuits blamed the Commandants at the fort, complaining that the Commandants hindered the progress of the missions, conspired to keep the Native Americans and other French away from the Jesuits and were involved in illegal activities. Carheil even stated that one of the Commandants had fathered a child in St. Ignace.

LAWLESS MACKINAC

Was it even possible to survive in New France while abiding by the many excessive, ridiculous laws imposed by French officials?

The coureurs de bois, voyagers, soldiers and commandants at Michilimackinac were all accused of lawlessness and illegal activities. Many of the major leaders, including but not limited to the commandants at the fort, were charged with or accused of crimes. Several leaders, including Cadillac, eventually ended their careers as prison inmates. LaSalle became a victim of homicide. Many others were victims of disease, alcohol or war.

Lawlessness traveled to other areas of the colony as the French moved with the fur trade. Detroit, which was founded by people from St. Ignace, was plagued with accusations and bickering.

Cadillac's Lieutenant, Alphonse de Tonty,[82] who was probably the last commander at Fort de Buade, relocated to Detroit. He disagreed with Cadillac who accused him of conspiring with the Jesuits to rebuild a fort at Michilimackinac. Later, charges were pressed by Cadillac against Alphonse de Tonty for embezzlement and engaging in illegal fur trading. He was not convicted and turned the tables against Cadillac. This rift eventually led to strife for Cadillac, who was sued by de Tonty. Cadillac was temporarily banned from Fort Pontchartrain, the settlement he created. This suspension of Cadillac's powers led the colonial government to void all of the deeds conveyed by Cadillac in newly formed Detroit. The instability caused a decline in population at the fort. Eventually the French government had to resort to bribery to lure habitants to Detroit. Each family was offered a cow, a pig, a wagon and land.

An arsonist burned Fort Pontchartrain, de Tonty and Cadillac's homes, the Recollet Priest's house, a barn, the church and all the food stores for the French. This left the French at the mercy of the local Native American population for food. Soon after, a group of Miami attacked the Native Americans at Detroit. A short time later, a group of Illinois that were bent on attacking were captured. In 1712, thirteen hundred Mascouten were determined to attack Detroit. Only 30 French soldiers were at the fort to fight them off. All buildings outside of Fort Detroit, including the church and Cadillac's house, were burned by the French. This was done to eliminate hiding places for the attackers.

Eventually, Cadillac's management of Fort Pontchartrain and the settlement was investigated by the government. The results were less than flattering. The report concluded that Fort Detroit was rotting and poorly designed. It also concluded that Cadillac was a bully who withheld food from the soldiers and profited in brandy. The report concluded by stating that the settlement and fort were a burden to the whole colony of Canada. Oddly, in the end, Cadillac was promoted and removed from the Great Lakes to Louisiana where he was named Governor.

Cadillac who was often described as boastful, opinionated and ingenious was recalled from his appointment as Governor of Louisiana in 1715. He was investigated, fined for using brandy as a trade item and jailed for six months. Later he was released and received another governorship in France.

Cadillac was sued for underhanded business practices by traders that he employed. When he and traders disagreed about the way that trading was being carried out, Cadillac had them imprisoned at St. Ignace. Cadillac ordered soldiers from the garrison to break into the trader's cabins to seize guns, lead and powder, food, blankets, salt and pepper, playing cards and many other items. These were items that had been received in trade for brandy that was sold at St. Ignace. Cadillac has been accused by historians of keeping the items for his personal use. Canadian laws were eventually established due to Cadillac's activities. Those laws defined the ownership of private property and prevented seizure of that property by those other than the courts.

Mrs. Cadillac testified during these trials; her testimony was found to lack credibility. She was rumored to have engaged in unlicensed trade at Mackinac prior to arriving in Detroit. If true, this would indicate that the first European woman in Michigan arrived at St. Ignace, not Detroit, as history books report.

Cadillac and Alphonse de Tonty were not the only Fort de Buade commanders accused of criminal activity. Louis de La Porte de Louvigny, Commandant of Fort de Buade in the 1690s, was tried in 1699 for illegal trading. He was convicted of "commercial transactions and contravening the orders of the King".[83]

Daniel Greysolon Duluth, who was Commandant of Fort de Buade in the 1680s, was referred to as "King of the Outlaws". Duluth's business ventures were well known and he possibly plotted these illegal activities with Governor Frontenac. A historic unsigned letter believed to be from Frontenac seemingly blessed Duluth's illegal trading, indicating that the author's philosophy was that what others did not know would not hurt them.[84]

Famous explorers, including LaSalle and those who consorted with or were employed by him, were also accused of insidious activities. LaSalle, on at least two occasions, had mass desertions and thefts by his crews. In both cases Michilimackinac played a part in the lawless activities.

In advance of LaSalle's first voyage to Michilimackinac he sent a crew to trade for supplies. On his arrival in the *Griffin* he found the men had deserted, taking the trade goods with them.

Later, a different group of men stole his provisions, ammunition and trade goods. They demolished and abandoned LaSalle's fort on the Miami River. These criminals also went to St. Ignace and seized the furs stored there by LaSalle. These actions left LaSalle in poor financial condition and almost cost Henri de Tonty and his remaining men their lives.

LaSalle continued to explore amidst financial difficulties. His expedition parties reached as far as Texas, prior to LaSalle being murdered by his own men.

The Jesuits and LaSalle also had an ongoing feud. LaSalle accused the Jesuits of trading more in furs than souls and providing the Native Americans with liquor. Meanwhile, the Jesuits accused LaSalle of being mad, fit only for an insane asylum. This ongoing feud led to lobbying to have Joliet explore the West instead of LaSalle.

Nicholas Perrot dit Turbal, also known as Joly Coeur, was the man who claimed the western Great Lakes for France. He had often been the go-to person for France, respected by Native tribes, Jesuits and French alike. Perrot had gathered Native Americans to help capture English and Dutch expeditions who attacked Michilimackinac in the 1680s. Instead of recognizing his efforts he was later branded an illegal trader.

Perrot was accused, then admitted to attempting to murder LaSalle by preparing him a poisoned salad. Perrot named the Jesuits in his confession, stating they had employed him to poison LaSalle. LaSalle, who mistrusted the Jesuits greatly, forgave Perrot and did not believe the Jesuits had any responsibility in the poisoning. Rather than have Perrot arrested and tried, he banished him.

Joliet continued to explore and eventually was rewarded with the title Hydrographer to the King. He was given the Island of Anticosta in the St. Lawrence River, the world's largest privately owned island. He suffered great losses of property during the war with the English.

Joliet's schoolmate and traveling companion, Marquette, seems to be one of the few original explorers of Michilimack-inac whose reputation was unscathed. Marquette, beloved by the Native Americans of the times, went down in history without a traceable negative word written about his life. He is the namesake of various places in Michigan and the Midwest.

Other religious icons of Mackinac went down in history with less flattering reputations. Hennepin, the Recollet missionary who traveled with LaSalle, was noted in history as a controversial liar. He died in Italy in 1705 after being threatened with imprisonment by Louis XIV. His memoirs are often criticized by historians as plagiarized, inflated and boastful misrepresentations.

Based on the viewpoints of Cadillac, Jesuit Etienne Carheil was disliked. Cadillac accused him of hiding his true motivations. He was called domineering and was said to have disobeyed Cadillac. On one occasion he threatened to hit the Commandant.[85] The other Jesuits found him to be brilliant; he was responsible for writing a textbook on the Huron language.

In the early 1700s, the Jesuits were banned from Detroit. Cadillac accused the Jesuits at Michilimackinac of concealing stolen furs taken from warehouses in Detroit. By the mid 1700s, the Jesuits had begun loosing political favor. In 1762 the Jesuits were expelled from France by the parliament.

AFTER

Michilimackinac became less the capital of the freshwater world and more of a supply base. It was noted as a staging area for western expeditions in the 1700s. One reference identified Michilimackinac as the "Grand Depot" and Green Bay and LaPointe, Wisconsin were identified as secondary supply depots.

After the removal of the garrison to Fort Detroit and the burning of the chapel by the Jesuits between 1703 and 1706, St. Ignace continued to serve as a trading post and religious center for a time. The missionaries became more transient, wandering from Native American camp to Native American camp.

Most of the Huron and some of the Odawa moved to Detroit. Some Odawa believed Cadillac had the ability to place a curse on those who did not follow him. Many went to Detroit to avoid untimely deaths. Other Odawa moved to the Isle of Castor which is presently known as Beaver Island.

Officially the French era at Michilimackinac had begun its decline. However, the French and Native American people who were outside the government did not see this. Charles Junchereau de Saint Denys was given permission to build a tannery at St. Ignace. In 1702 he headed for Michilimackinac with goods and a party of Frenchmen, including de Tonty and a wealthy trader named La Forest. The license did not allow Junchereau to trade fur and he immediately got into trouble. Finding that the French at Michilimackinac would not take his goods in trade for provisions; he was forced to trade the goods to Native Americans for beaver skins to pay his tab. He later defended his actions by pointing out the overall lawlessness of Michilimackinac, attempting to shift the blame to others who broke the rules.

In the early 1700s, the French realized that the removal of the garrison had been a mistake. The northern door to the fur trade was left open. Though the fur itself was depleted in the eastern Great Lakes, the pathway to its import from the west necessitated traveling through the Straits of Mackinac or down the St. Mary's River.[86] Immediately after moving the garrison to Detroit, Francois Clairambault D'Aigrement, an inspector for the French Government who stayed at Michilimackinac for several days in 1708, found only about 15 Frenchmen remained. They busied themselves with smuggling liquor and trading it for furs.

Only 25 Huron remained at Michilimackinac. The rest of the Huron and some of the Chippewa had abandoned Michilimackinac for Detroit. They joined Cadillac, the Miami, the Fox and other tribes. Too much togetherness at Fort Detroit soon inflamed hostilities between the Native Americans.

Records indicate that one of the four Odawa Tribes, the Sable Odawa, left for Detroit temporarily but returned after involvement in ambushing and killing the Miami at Detroit in 1706. The attack went awry. Among the 83 dead were a

French priest and two French soldiers. Cadillac imprisoned Odawa Chief La Pesant (French for Fat One), ordering him to stand trial. Somehow, much to the amazement of all who commented on the Chief's advanced age and bulging mid-section, he scaled the palisade wall and canoed back to Michilimackinac.

Around 1712 an estimated 40 coureurs de bois, labeled by Father Marest as "deserters who were only out for their own interests," remained in St. Ignace. The French rebuilt the fort on the Mackinaw City side of the Straits soon after.

When Father Charlevoix visited St. Ignace (which he referred to as North Michilimackinac) in 1721, he found a mid-sized village where the beaver trade continued at a great pace. The fort and missionary living quarters were still in existence. "The fort is still kept up as well as the house of the missionaries, who at present are not distressed with business, having never found the Outawaies much disposed to receive their instructions."[87] The fort was, in fact, reinforced after a siege by the local Native Americans in 1706.[88]

The Odawa, the last holdouts who had resolved to Father Joseph J. Marest to die at Michilimackinac, eventually moved across the Straits. This move was probably around 1740, prompted by exhausted soil at Michilimackinac. This move was across the Straits to L'Arbre Croche or Mackinaw City, or possibly from St. Ignace to Mackinaw City sometime in the early 1700s and then to L'Arbre Croche. In *Mackinac, Formerly Michilimackinac*, Lt. Col. John R. Bailey concludes, "The movement to South Michilimackinac must have been gradual up to 1760, when the province of Michilimackinac was transferred to the English."[89]

In 1760 the French lost Montreal and then all of New France to the British. Fort Michilimackinac in Mackinaw City was occupied by the British in 1761. The French, who had occupied the land for more than a century, continued to populate homes around the Great Lakes. Many of them lived with their Metis families. According to English fur trader Alexander Henry, former French soldiers occupied a majority of homes in Fort Michilimackinac. Retired voyagers also resided in the Michilimackinac area.

The French continued to side with the Native Americans against the English. Their fur trading continued. They set up rough establishments along canoe routes. They traded maple sugar, wild rice, everything and anything. They performed canoe repairs, collecting birch bark and resins for the repairs. They baked and sold bread. They ran restaurants and opened taverns. They continued to trade in fur and were known to bring thousands of muskrats to the English market in Detroit. After the fall of the English, the French continued to supply fur to the Americans. They acted as market hunters and traded venison.

At the close of the French colonial period in 1763, the population of New France (Canada) was estimated to be 100,000, one tenth of the population of New England. This estimate included 30,000 Native Americans and 400 black slaves.

Footnotes

[1]E.B. O'Callaghan and John Romeyn Brodhead. *New York Colonial Documents*. Vol. IX. Albany: Weed, Parsons and Company, 1855. 383.

[2]John Read Bailey. *Mackinac: Formerly Michilimackinac*. Lansing: D. D. Thorp, 1896. 80.

[3]The de Tontys and Duluth were cousins.

[4] The term for racially mixed Native American and French.

[5]Stephen de Carheil was a vocal opponent of Cadillac, complaining about the poor influence the garrison and its leaders had on the Native American population at Michilimackinac.

[6]Antoine Laumet de la Mothe Cadillac. *Cadillac's Papers, Historical Collections of the Michigan Pioneer and Historical Society*. 33, 1904. 162.

[7]Archaeological evidence proves there was a Native American presence at Michilimackinac for three or four thousand years prior to the arrival of the first French in the 1600s. Burials found on the south side of St. Ignace date to the Late Archaic period, ca. 4,500 to 3,000 before present. However, most of the remains found in the St. Ignace area date to the Middle Woodland era, ca. 2,400 to 1,400 before

present. This would include burials found on North and South State Streets, Huron Avenue and other areas of St. Ignace and the region. Late Woodland sites dating from approximately a.d. 600 have been found in Mackinac County in various places along the Lake Michigan and Huron shores.

[8]"...sacrifice consists of throwing into the water tobacco, provisions and kettles; and in asking him that the water of the river may flow more slowly, that the rocks may not break their canoes and that he will grant them an abundant catch."

Jesuit Relations 67, Thwaites Translation. Native Americans also tied together the legs of dogs and sacrificed them to stacks (Rabbit's Back) by throwing them in Lake Huron.

[9]Scholars believe it possible that the first human presence in the Great Lakes followed the retreat of the glaciers 10,000 years ago. Evidence has been found in the Lower Peninsula where spear points have been embedded in ancient mastodon bones.

[10]The Dakota are also known as the Sioux or Lakota.

[11]Reuben Gold Thwaites, ed. *Jesuit Relations and Allied Documents* 59. Cleveland: Burrows Bros., 1899. 201.

[12]James Alvin Van Fleet. *Old and New Mackinac: With Copious Extracts...* Ann Arbor: Courier Steam Printing-House, 1870. 63. Statements by Cadillac regarding St. Ignace.

[13]Ibid.

[14]Allow the author to apologize for the sometimes crude, blunt and misinformed statements of the explorers, soldiers and Jesuits. As the book is meant to explore the Wild West

conditions of the region, it is a believed necessity that the reader be aware of the impact of the cultural mix. Information may be included which might offend some readers, especially if they judge the prior residents based on what is the cultural norm today. Quotes from the period which may initially appear insensitive may also serve as an example of just how insensitive or misinformed the various participants of the time were. These quotes reveal how the newly intermingled Jesuits, explorers, traders and Natives really were only living and existing in one location, not blending and becoming one.

[15]Nine miles.

[16]Ibid.

[17]James T. Carney. *Berrien Bi-centennial*. Benton Harbor: Berrien County Bicentennial Commission, 1976. 35.

[18]M. A. Lesson. *The Recent Discoveries at St. Ignace. Shall We, or Shall We Not, Recover the Bones of Marquette-Correspondence of the Evening News*. Mackinac, July 12, 1877. History of Macomb County, Michigan: Containing an Account of Its Settlement, Growth, Development and Resources…, Chicago: M. A. Leeson and Co., 1882. 31.

[19]Will Connelly. *Downriver Michigan, Ice Age to Today*. Connelly Co., 1976. 14.

[20]Per *Before the Bridge*, Mackinac Island was not settled for 100 years after Marquette settled in St. Ignace. Limits on game and unsafe weather conditions were thought to be some of the reasons that the Native Americans avoided settling on islands. Some historians also believe the relatively shallow depth of the soil on Mackinac Island was a catalyst to settlement on the site of St. Ignace.

[21]Henry Rowe Schoolcraft. *Personal Memoirs of a Residence of Thirty Years with the Indian Tribes on the American Frontiers*. Philadelphia: Lippincott, Grambo and Co., 1851. 80.

[22]Bruce Catton. *Michigan, A History*. New York: W.W. Norton & Company, 1984. 12.

[23]Henry Rowe Schoolcraft. *Personal Memoirs of a Residence of Thirty Years with the Indian Tribes on the American Frontiers*. Philadelphia: Lippincott, Grambo and Co., 1851. 230.

[24]M.A. Lesson. The Recent Discoveries at St. Ignace. *Shall We, or Shall We Not, Recover the Bones of Marquette-Correspondence of the Evening News*. Mackinac, July 12, 1877, History of Macomb County, Michigan: Containing an Account of Its Settlement, Growth, Development and Resources…, Chicago: M.A. Lesson and Co., 1882. 31.

[25]Reuben Gold Thwaites, ed. *The Jesuit Relations 61*. Cleveland: Burrows Brothers, 1899. 121.

[26]Reuben Gold Thwaites, ed. *The Jesuit Relations 61*. Cleveland: Burrows Brothers, 1899. 123.

[27]John Gilmary Shea. *Shea's Discovery and Exploration of the Mississippi Valley*. New York: Redfield, 1853. 49.

[28]Reuben Gold Thwaites, ed. *The Jesuit Relations 61*. Cleveland: Burrows Brothers, 1899, 131-133.

[29]Reuben Gold Thwaites, ed. *The Jesuit Relations 61*. Cleveland: Burrows Brothers, 1899. 137-143.

[30]Reuben Gold Thwaites, ed. *The Jesuit Relations 62*. Cleveland: Burrows Brothers, 1900. 191.

[31]The 40 acre parcel lying at the mouth of the Moran River, crossing the roadway known as U.S.2.

[32]Emerson Smith. *Before the Bridge*. Kiwanis Club of St. Ignace, 1957. 43.

[33]Emerson Smith. *Before the Bridge*. Kiwanis Club of St. Ignace, 1957. 42.

[34]Dwight H. Kelton. *Annals of Fort Mackinac*. Detroit: Detroit Free Press, 1886. 15.

[35]John Read Bailey. *Mackinac: Formerly Michilimackinac*. Lansing: D. D. Thorp, 1896. 59.

[36]Reuben Gold Thwaites, ed. *The Jesuit Relations 62*. Cleveland: Burrows Brothers, 1900. 225.

[37]William Bennett Munro. *Crusaders of New France- A Chronicle of the Fleur-de-Lis in the Wilderness*. New Haven: Yale University Press, 1918. 11.

[38]A square arpent is about .844 of a square acre.

[39]Reuben Gold Thwaites, ed. *New Voyages to North America by the Baron de Lahontan*. Chicago: A.C. McClurg & Co., 1905. 94.

[40]Regarding Jesuit Father Jean de Breboeuf who was killed by the Iroquois. John McClelland Bulkley. *History of Monroe County, Michigan*. Chicago: Lewis Publishing Co., 1913. 4.

[41]Henry Rowe Schoolcraft. *Personal Memoirs of a Residence of Thirty Years*. Philadelphia: Lippincott, Grambo and Co., 1851. 102.

[42]Pierre Francois Xavier de Charlevoix. *Charlevoix Journal of a Voyage to North America*. Chicago: The Caxton Club, 1942. 45.

[43]Most historians contend that Marie Therese Guyon (Mrs. Cadillac) and Mrs. Alphonse de Tonty were the first European women in Michigan, taking up residence in Detroit in 1702. It can be questioned, however, whether Marie Therese Guyon spent time at St. Ignace prior to residing at Detroit. Some historians believe she made a trip to St. Ignace, prior to her trip to Detroit; in order to find and transport a store of brandy which had been hidden there by her husband.

[44]The history of the founding of Detroit is extremely important to the history of early Michilimackinac. The French left St. Ignace and founded Detroit. The same family lines were then responsible for the early government of New Orleans. Many of the French soldiers and coureurs de bois remained in the Great Lakes and Michilimackinac area. Those families were responsible for founding Grand Rapids, Green Bay, occupying the Saginaw Valley and founding Chicago. Many street names in Detroit, etc. are named from the early French, some of which came from St. Ignace. One can also assume that descriptions of early life in Detroit coincide with what would be described regarding Michilimackinac if more written records existed.

[45]John Read Bailey. *Mackinac: Formerly Michilimackinac*. Lansing: D. D. Thorp, 1896. 53-54.

[46]Milo Quaife, ed. *The Western Country in the 17th Century: Memoirs of Lamothe Cadillac and Pierre Liette*. Chicago: The Lakeside Press, 1947. 3.

[47]John Read Bailey. *Mackinac: Formerly Michilimackinac.* Lansing: D. D. Thorp, 1896. 52.

[48]"Vide Poche" means empty pockets.

[49]Dwight H. Kelton. *Annals of Fort Mackinac.* Detroit: Detroit Free Press, 1886. 166.

[50]Electa Maria Sheldon. *The Early History of Michigan: From the First Settlement to 1815.* New York: A.S. Barnes & Co., 1856. 287.

[51]Henry Rowe Schoolcraft. *Personal Memoirs of a Residence of Thirty Years with the Indian Tribes on the American Frontiers.* Philadelphia: Lippincott, Grambo and Co., 1851. 123.

[52]Dirk Gringhuis. *Moccasin Tracks, A Saga of the Michigan Indian.* Lansing: Michigan State University, 1974. 21.

[53]Reuben Gold Thwaites, ed. *New Voyages to North America by the Baron de Lahontan.* Chicago: A.C. McClurg & Co., 1905. 109.

[54]Lucy and Sidney Corbett. *French Cooking in Old Detroit Since 1701.* Detroit: Wayne University Press, 1951. 2.

[55]Reuben Gold Thwaites, ed. *New Voyages to North America by the Baron de Lahontan.* Chicago: A.C. McClurg & Co., 1905. 115.

[56]John Gilmary Shea. *Shea's Discovery and Exploration of the Mississippi Valley.* New York: Redfield, 1853. 24.

[57]James T. Carney. *Berrien Bi-centennial.* Benton Harbor: Berrien County Bicentennial Commission, 1976. 34.

[58]Meade C. Williams. *Early Mackinac: A Sketch, Historical and Descriptive.* St. Louis: Buschart Brothers, 1901. 24.

[59]Tribes from the Great Lakes included Odawa, Chippewa, Menominee, Huron, Pottawatomie, Bone (Assiboin) Indians, Illinois, Miami, Cree, Monsoni, Winnebago, Fox, Sioux, Sacs or Sauk and Nippising.

[60]Theodore C. Pease and Raymond C. Werner, eds. *The French Foundations, 1680-1693, Collections of the Illinois State Historical Library*, Vol. 23. Springfield: Illinois State Historical Library, 1934. 15.

[61]Henry Rowe Schoolcraft. *Personal Memoirs of a Residence of Thirty Years with the Indian Tribes on the American Frontiers*. Philadelphia: Lippincott, Grambo and Co., 1851. 274.

[62]Henry Rowe Schoolcraft. *Personal Memoirs of a Residence of Thirty Years with the Indian Tribes on the American Frontiers*. Philadelphia: Lippincott, Grambo and Co., 1851. 101.

[63]Francis Parkman. *Count Frontenac and New France under Louis XIV*. Toronto: George Morang and Company, 1899. 91.

[64]Reuben Gold Thwaites, ed. *Jesuit Relations and Allied Documents 54*. Cleveland: Burrows Bros., 1899. 145.

[65]Henry Rowe Schoolcraft. *Personal Memoirs of a Residence of Thirty Years with the Indian Tribes on the American Frontiers*. Philadelphia: Lippincott, Grambo and Co., 1851. 139.

[66]Reuben Gold Thwaites, ed. *Jesuit Relations and Allied Documents 67*. Cleveland: Burrows Bros., 1899. 153.

[67]Francis Parkman. *LaSalle and the Discovery of the Great West*. Boston: Little, Brown & Co., 1905. 153.

[68]Francis Parkman. *LaSalle and the Discovery of the Great West*. Boston: Little, Brown & Co., 1905. 154-155.

[69]Agnes C. Laut. *Cadillac*. Indianapolis: Bobbs, Merrill, 1931. 55.

[70]Agnes C. Laut. *Cadillac*. Indianapolis: Bobbs, Merrill, 1931. 55.

[71]Emerson Smith. *Before the Bridge*. Kiwanis Club of St. Ignace, 1957. 42-43.

[72]Reuben Gold Thwaites, ed. *The Jesuit Relations 55*. Cleveland: Burrows Brothers, 1899. 157.

[73]Reuben Gold Thwaites, ed. *Jesuit Relations and Allied Documents 5*. Cleveland: Burrows Bros., 1899. 125. Statement made by Father Paul le Jeune.

[74]John Gilmary Shea. *Shea's Discovery and Exploration of the Mississippi Valley*. New York: Redfield, 1853. 23.

[75]Electa Maria Sheldon. *Early History of Michigan: From the First Settlement to 1815*. New York: A.S. Barnes and Co., 1856. 72.

[76]Electa Maria Sheldon. *Early History of Michigan: From the First Settlement to 1815*. New York: A.S. Barnes and Co., 1856. 73-80.

[77]Agnes Laut. *Cadillac*. Indianapolis: The Bobb-Merrill Co., 1931. 111.

[78]Roger Andrews. *Old Fort Mackinac on the Hill of History*. Menominee: Herald-Leader Press, 1938. 19.

[79]Francis Parkman. *Count Frontenac and New France under Louis XIV*. Toronto: George Morang and Company, 1899. 95.

[80]Reuben Gold Thwaites, ed. *Jesuit Relations and Allied Documents 65*. Cleveland: Burrows Bros., 1899. 197.

[81]Reuben Gold Thwaites, ed. *Jesuit Relations and Allied Documents 65*. Cleveland: Burrows Bros., 1899. 193.

[82]De Tonty became commander of Fort Pontchartrain in 1720.

[83]Electa Maria Sheldon. *The Early History of Michigan: From the First Settlement to 1815*. New York: A.S. Barnes & Co., 1856. 189.

[84]Electa Maria Sheldon. *The Early History of Michigan: From the First Settlement to 1815*. New York: A.S. Barnes & Co., 1856. 62-63.

[85]Francis Parkman. *Parkman's Works*. Boston: Little, Brown & Co., 1905. 20.

[86]By the mid-1700s, the French at Fort Detroit numbered only twenty.

[87]Edwin Orin Wood. *Historic Mackinac*. New York: Macmillan Co., 1918. 88.

[88]Electa Maria Sheldon. *The Early History of Michigan: From the First Settlement to 1815*. New York: A.S. Barnes & Co., 1856. 211.

[89]John Read Bailey. *Mackinac: Formerly Michilimackinac*. Lansing: D. D. Thorp, 1896. 73.

Sources

Andrews, Roger. *Old Fort Mackinac on the Hill of History*. Herald-Leader Press, 1938. 19.

Bailey, John Read. *Mackinac: Formerly Michilimackinac*, D.D. Thorp, 1896. 59,73,80.

Bulkley, John McClelland. *History of Monroe County, Michigan*, Chicago: Lewis Publishing Co. 1913. 4.

Cadillac, Antoine Laumet de la Mothe. *Cadillac's Papers. Historical Collections of the Michigan Pioneer and Historical Society*, 33 (1904), 162.

Carney, James T. *Berrien. Bi-centennial. Berrien County Bicentennial Commission*, 1976. 34-35.

Catton, Bruce. *Michigan, A History*. W. W. Norton & Company, 1984. 12.

Charlevoix, Pierre Francois Xavier de. *Journal of a Voyage to North America*. Caxton Club, 1942. 45.

Connelly, Will. *Downriver Michigan*, Ice Age to Today. Connelly Co., 1976. 12.

Corbett, Lucy and Sidney. *French Cooking in Old Detroit Since 1701*. Detroit: Wayne University Press, 1951. 2, 81.

Corbett, Lucy and Sidney. *Pot Shots from a Grosse Ile Kitchen*. New York: Harper & Brothers Publishers, 1947.

Costain, Thomas B. *The White and the Gold: The French Regime in Canada*. Garden City: The Country Life Press, 1954.

Gringhuis, Dirk. *Moccasin Tracks, A Saga of the Michigan Indian*. Lansing: Michigan State University, 1974. 21.

Kelton, Dwight H. *Annals of Fort Mackinac*. Detroit Free Press, 1886. 15.

Laut, Agnes C. *Cadillac*. Indianapolis: Bobbs, Merrill, 1931. 55, 111, 136.

Munro, William Bennett. *Crusaders of New France-A Chronicle of the Fleur-de-Lis in the Wilderness*, Yale University Press, (1918), 11.

O'Callaghan, E. B. and John Romeyn Brodhead. *New York Colonial Documents IX*. Albany: Weed, Parsons and Company, 1855. Various.

Parkman, Francis. *Count Frontenac and New France under Louis XIV*. Toronto: George Morang and Company, 1899. 91, 95.

Parkman, Francis. *LaSalle and the Discovery of the Great West*. Boston: Little, Brown & Co., 1905. 153-155.

Parkman, Francis. *Parkman's Works*. Boston: Little, Brown & Co., 1905. 20.

Pease, Theodore C. and Raymond C. Werner, eds. *The French Foundations, 1680-1693*. Collections of the Illinois State

Historical Library, vol. 23., Springfield: Illinois State Historical Library, 1934. 15.

Quaife, Milo, ed. *The Western Country in the 17th Century: Memoirs of Lamothe Cadillac and Pierre Liette*. Chicago: The Lakeside Press, 1947. 3.

Schoolcraft, Henry Rowe. *Personal Memoirs of a Residence of Thirty Years with the Indian Tribes on the American Frontiers*. Philadelphia, Lippincott, Grambo and Co., 1851. 80, 101, 123, 130, 139, 230, 274. http://memory.loc.gov/cgi-bin/query/r?ammem/lhbum:@fieldDCICID+@lit(lhbum150 06div16)). (Accessed 2007-2010.)

Sheldon, Electa Maria. *The Early History of Michigan: From the First Settlement to 1815*. New York: A.S. Barnes & Co., 1856. 62-63, 72-80, 189, 211, 287.

Shea, John Gilmary. *Shea's Discovery and Exploration of the Mississippi Valley*. Redfield, 1853. 23-24, 49, 155.

Shea, John Gilmary. *History of the Catholic Church within the Limits of the United States*. New York, 1890.

Smith, Emerson. *Before the Bridge*. Kiwanis Club of St. Ignace, 1957. Various.

Thwaites, Reuben Gold, ed. *Jesuit Relations and Allied Documents, 1610-1791*. 73 Volumes, Burrows Bros., 1896-1901. Various.

Thwaites, Reuben Gold, ed. *New Voyages to North America by the Baron de Lahontan*. Chicago: A. C. McClurg & Co., 1905. 94, 109, 115.

Van Fleet, James Alvin. *Old and New Mackinac: With Copious Extracts…* Courier Steam Printing House, 1870. 63.

Williams, Meade C. *Early Mackinac: A Sketch, Historical and Descriptive*. St. Louis: Buschart Brothers, 1901. 24.

Wood, Edwin Orin. *Historic Mackinac*. New York: Macmillan Co., 1918. 88.